The Pasta
Machine
Cook Book

Gabriella Mari
Cristina Blasi

The Pasta Machine Cook Book

McRae BOOKS

ISBN 88-89272-42-2

This book was conceived, edited and designed by McRae Books Srl

Borgo Santa Croce, 8 – 50122 Florence, Italy

info@mcraebooks.com

Project Director: Anne McRae

Design Director: Marco Nardi

Text: Scuola di Arte Culinaria Cordon Bleu (Gabriella Mari, Cristina Blasi)

Home Economists: Gabriella Mari, Cristina Blasi, Emila Onesti

Photography: Marco Lanza

Layouts: Sara Mathews

Editing: Anne McRae

Color separations: Fotolito Toscana, Florence

Printed in Slovakia

Contents

Flavors of spring spinach tagliatelle

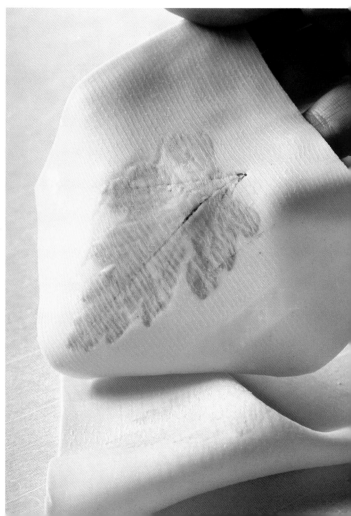

Introduction

Preparing pasta at home is a lot simpler than you may think. In these first few pages we have explained how to make pasta dough and how to roll it through a machine to achieve the desired thickness. For those without a pasta machine, or with a hankering for perfection, we have also explained how to roll pasta by hand. Cutting pasta is simple and we have explained how to do it both by hand and using a machine.

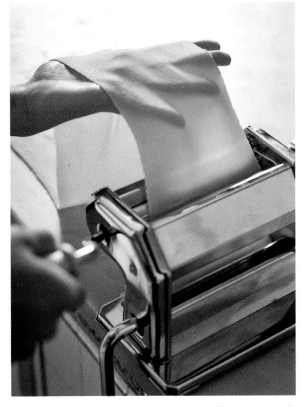

Above: Rolling the dough
Left: Preparing pasta with stripes and motifs

With its delicate texture and flavor, homemade pasta is a unique ingredient that requires special care and attention in the making. The first thing you will notice is that even if you make pasta often, some days the dough will require less flour or more kneading, or other small changes to the basic method. Even slight variations in temperature and humidity, or in your own mood, will affect the outcome. For this reason we strongly suggest that you always mix and knead the dough by hand and then cut it using the machine. This will allow you to modify the dough each time, correcting the amount of flour or egg and judging the time required for kneading.

Plain pasta is made with unbleached or all-purpose, plain flour, but many other types of flour can be used. Each one will require more or less liquid; refer to the chart below for quantities and then adjust them as you work. Kneading time will also vary depending on the flour you use. Soft-wheat flour has less gluten and takes the longest time to knead, generally about 20 minutes. Hard-wheat flour will take about half that time.

With regard to quantity, in Italy we normally allow about $3^1/_2$ oz (100 g) of fresh pasta per person. This can be obtained using $3^1/_2$ oz (100 g) of flour and 1 large egg. As the pasta dries it will lose a little weight. You should also remember that in Italy we serve pasta as a first course, to be followed by an often substantial second course. If you are serving pasta as the main part of the meal, then you should double the quantities.

Always cook fresh pasta in a large pan of already salted, boiling water. For every $3^1/_2$ oz (100 g) of pasta you should allow 1 quart (1 liter) of water and $1^1/_2$ teaspoons of coarse sea salt. If the pasta has become very dry it is better to add the salt after the pasta, when the water returns to a boil. Cooking times depend on the shape and thickness of the pasta. Simple ribbon pasta rolled through the machine at the thinnest setting will only require 2 minutes to cook. Thicker or filled pasta such as tortellini will require a few minutes more.

Many types of fresh pasta can be frozen. Lay the nests of ribbon pasta or single pieces of filled pasta well spaced on a large tray and place in the freezer. Transfer to bags as soon as they are frozen and seal well. Filled pasta with potato filling is not suited to freezing. Baked pasta can be prepared up to just before going into the oven. To thaw, remove from the freezer and place in a warm oven for 30 minutes, then bake.

Dough	All-purpose flour	Other flour	Eggs	Water	Other ingredients	Salt
Plain fresh pasta	$2^2/_3$ cups/400 g		4			
Durum or hard wheat pasta		$2^2/_3$ cups/400 g durum or hard wheat		$1^1/_4$ cups/ 300 ml		
Durum or hard wheat and egg pasta	$1^1/_3$ cups/200 g	$1^1/_3$ cups/200 g durum or hard wheat	4			
Ravioli pasta	$2^1/_3$ cups/350 g		3	2 tbsp		
Whole-wheat/wholemeal pasta	$1^1/_3$ cups/200 g	$1^1/_3$ cups/200 g whole-wheat	4			
Chestnut pasta	2 cups/300 g	$^2/_3$ cup/100 g chestnut	2	4 tbsp		1 pinch
Buckwheat pasta		2 cups/300 g buckwheat & $^2/_3$ cup/100 g durum or hard wheat		scant cup/ 200 ml		
Colored pasta (tomato, (spinach, Swiss chard, etc.)	$2^1/_3$ cups/350 g		3		$^1/_3$ cup/50 g purée	1 pinch
Aromatic (coffee, herb, chocolate, etc)	$2^1/_3$ cups/350 g		4		$^1/_3$ cup/50 g powder or minced herbs	
Black	$2^2/_3$ cups/400 g		3		1 tbsp squid's ink (about 3 sacs)	

Made in these proportions you will get about 14 oz (400 g) of fresh pasta which is enough to make basic ribbon pasta (tagliatelle, etc) for 4 people, or lasagne or filled pasta (ravioli, etc) for 8 people.

Preparing the dough

Plain fresh pasta is made of a simple mixture of artfully kneaded flour and eggs. In Italy, soft wheat "0" flour is used. All-purpose or plain white flour can be used in other parts of the world. Fresh pasta can also be made with hard wheat, buckwheat, chestnut, or other types of flour, and the eggs can be replaced with water, oil, or milk. Whatever the ingredients, the basic method is always the same.

Plain fresh pasta

Ingredients
- 2²⁄₃ cups/400 g all-purpose/plain flour
- 4 very fresh large eggs

❶

Sift the flour onto a clean work surface (preferably made of wood) and shape into a mound. Make a hollow in the center.

❷

Use a fork to beat the eggs lightly in a small bowl. Pour the beaten eggs into the hollow center of the mound of flour.

❸

Use the fork to gradually incorporate the eggs into the flour. Take care not to break the wall of flour or the eggs will run.

❹

When almost all the flour has been absorbed use your hands and, if you have one, a pasta scraper to gather the dough up into a ball.

❺

Wash and dry your hands and begin the kneading process. Place the dough on a clean work surface. At first it will be rough and grainy.

❻

Knead by pushing down and forward on the ball of pasta with the heel of your palm. Fold the dough in half, give it a quarter-turn, and repeat.

❼

As you work the dough will become smoother. The warmth of your hands and the rhythmic kneading creates a gluten-forming protein, which gives pasta its special texture.

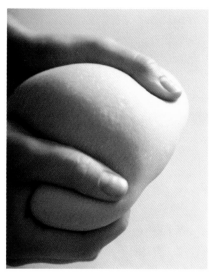

❽

After 10–20 minutes (depending on the flour being used), the dough should be smooth and silky, with tiny air bubbles visible on the surface. Wrap the dough in plastic wrap (cling film) and let rest for 30 minutes.

Rolling and cutting the dough by machine

If making simple ribbon pasta types, such as tagliatelle or lasagne, run all the sheets through the machine one notch at a time. This will give them time to dry a little before being rolled to the next thickness. If making stuffed pasta, such as ravioli, roll the pasta one sheet at a time to the thinnest setting and make the ravioli before rolling the next sheet. This will prevent the pasta from drying out too much.

Kneading time

This depends on the type of flour used, your kneading skill, and climatic conditions. Normally, soft wheat dough will require 20 minutes; a mixed soft and hard wheat dough will take 15 minutes; and hard wheat dough will be ready in just 10 minutes. Gentle, rhythmic kneading produces best results.

❶

Divide the dough into pieces (5–6 pieces for 14 oz/400 g of pasta, sufficient for 4 people).

❷

Roll a piece of dough through the machine at the thickest setting.

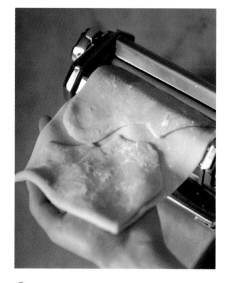

❸

Continue rolling the dough through the machine, reducing the thickness setting one notch at a time down to the required thickness. You may need to fold the pasta as you work to obtain an evenly shaped sheet.

4

The finished pasta sheets should be smooth and evenly shaped, without any folds. Extremely long sheets are difficult to manage; don't make them any longer than about 12–14 inches (30–35 cm).

5

Sprinkle the finished sheets with semolina and cover them with a clean dry cloth. This will allow them to dry a little before you begin to cut them.

6

To test the pasta to see if it is ready to cut, insert your index finger into a fold of pasta and pull slightly. If the pasta stretches it is not ready; if it tears, it is ready to cut.

7

Set the machine to the width required (for tagliolini, tagliatelle, pappardelle, etc.) and run each sheet through. If making ribbon pasta, gather the pasta up in your hand as it comes out of the machine and shape into little "nests."

Types of ribbon pasta

Classic Italian fresh ribbon pasta types are named according to their approximate width. The narrowest ribbons, taglierini or tagliolini, are about $1/4$ inch (5–6 mm) wide. Tagliatelle (also known as fettuccine) are normally about $1/2$ inch (1 cm) wide, while pappardelle measure about 1 inch (2.5–3 cm) in width.

Rolling the dough by hand

Pasta machines are ideal for new pasta makers, but as you gain in experience you may also wish to try rolling the pasta by hand. When properly done, hand-rolled pasta is better than the machine-rolled variety. Rolling by hand requires lots of energy and a large, flat work surface, preferably made of wood. You will also need a very long, rather thin rolling pin made especially for pasta.

❶

Unwrap the ball of pasta and use your fingertips to pull up a "button" or smaller ball of pasta on the top. This will keep the center piece of the pasta as thick as the edges when you roll.

❷

Put the ball of pasta on a large clean work surface. Place a very long pasta rolling pin on top and begin rolling from the center.

❸

Keep rolling the pasta by exerting an even pressure all along the length of the pin. Give the pasta a quarter-turn from time to time and keep working.

❹

Wrap the pasta around the rolling pin and continue rolling backward and forward, running your hands along the pin. When the sheet of pasta is as large as the work surface, let half of it drape over the edge of the table or board.

❺

Dust the finished sheets with semolina or coarsely ground cornmeal and cover with a clean dry cloth. This will allow them to dry a little before you begin to cut them.

❻

To test the pasta to see if it is ready to cut, insert your index finger into a fold of pasta and pull slightly. If the pasta stretches it is not ready; if it tears, it is ready to cut.

Cutting pasta by hand

Pasta machines can cut lasagne and all the simple ribbon pasta types, such as tagliatelle and pappardelle, but even if you do own a machine, you may want to cut some ribbon pasta shapes by hand to give them that special "homemade look." Always remember to let the pasta dry a little in a floured cloth before cutting.

❶

Lasagne: The pasta will come out of the machine in sheets measuring about 6 x 12 inches (14 x 30 cm). Cut into pieces measuring about 5 x 6 inches (13 x 15 cm).

❷

Ribbon pasta (pappardelle, tagliatelle, taglierini, tagliolini, etc): Place the pasta sheets on a clean work surface sprinkled with semolina or coarsely ground polenta and fold them into flat rolls. Leave a border of about 1 inch or so (2.5 cm) sticking out from the roll.

❸

Use a sharp knife to cut the ribbon pasta to the desired width. The narrowest ribbons, taglierini or tagliolini, are about $1/4$ inch (5–6 mm) wide. Tagliatelle (also known as fettuccine) are normally about $1/2$ inch (1 cm) wide, while pappardelle are 1 inch (2.5–3 cm) in width.

❹

To unfold the ribbon pasta, grasp 2 or 3 pieces of the pasta sticking out from the roll and lift them up. Shape into "nests" or lie in flat strips on a floured cloth.

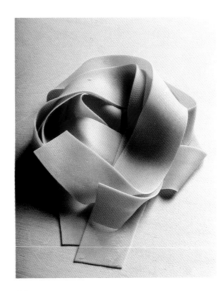

❺

Finished pappardelle can be quite wide.

Torn pasta, irregular cuts, and bows

Irregularly shaped pasta such as maltagliati (literally, "badly cut") will need to be cut by hand. Stracci (which translates as "rags") can be either cut with a knife or torn into irregular pieces by hand. Farfalle ("butterflies" or bows) are cut from strips and then pinched into shape.

❶

Stracci: Dust the pieces of pasta with semolina or coarsely ground cornmeal and gently tear or cut into irregular shapes.

❶

Maltagliati: Dust the pieces of pasta with semolina or coarsely ground cornmeal and cut into irregular diamond shapes or strips

Dusting fresh pasta

Always use coarsely ground semolina or cornmeal to dust the work surface or the finished pasta sheets or strips. The high starch content of these grains will stop the pasta from sticking much more effectively than finely ground flours.

❶

Bows: Use a fluted pastry cutter to cut the sheets of pasta into 1 x 2^1/$_2$-inch (2.5 x 6 cm) rectangles.

❷

Use the tips of your index finger and thumb to pinch each rectangle together in the center.

❸

Repeat until all the rectangles have been pinched into bows.

Garganelli

Garganelli are a type of rolled fresh pasta from Romagna in central Italy. They are named for their resemblance to a chicken's oesophagus ("*garganel*" in the Romagnese dialect). Garganelli are made by wrapping small squares of dough around a rod and running them over a special cane loom or comb.

Garganelli
Ingredients

- 2²/₃ cups/400 g all-purpose/plain flour
- 4 very fresh large eggs
- pinch of freshly grated nutmeg (optional)
- 4 tablespoons freshly grated Parmesan cheese

Prepare the pasta dough following the instructions on page 9, adding the nutmeg and Parmesan to the eggs. Wrap the dough in plastic wrap and let rest for 30 minutes. Divide the dough into 6 pieces. Roll it through the machine one notch at a time down to the second thinnest setting. Proceed as in step 1.

❶

Use a plain pastry cutter to cut the sheets of pasta in 1¹/₂-inch (3.5-cm) squares.

❷

Beginning with one pointed end, wrap each square of pasta around a rod about the thickness of a pencil or a very thick knitting needle. Roll each garganello lightly over the special comb to seal and make the ridges.

❸

Slip each garganello off the rod, resting them on a clean work surface dusted with semolina or coarsely ground cornmeal.

❹

Let the garganelli dry a little before cooking.

Saffron garganelli

Make bright yellow or red garganelli by adding 1/2 teaspoon of powdered saffron to the dough. In some versions, finely grated lemon zest is added to the eggs for extra flavor.

Aromatic pasta

Fresh pasta can be colored and flavored with many different dry ingredients, including cocoa powder, coffee, and finely chopped herbs. The basic method is the same as for plain fresh pasta (page 9). Cocoa powder can be sifted with the flour, while coffee and herbs can be added to the egg mixture.

(page 9)

Sauces for aromatic pasta

Choosing the sauce for aromatic pasta can be slightly more complicated than for plain pasta. Since the pasta itself is flavored the sauce should either complement or highlight its special taste.

Chocolate pasta

Ingredients

- 2 1/3 cups/350 g all-purpose/plain flour
- 1/3 cup/50 g unsweetened cocoa powder
- 3 very fresh large eggs

❶ Sift the flour and cocoa powder onto a clean work surface (preferably made of wood) and shape into a mound. Make a hollow in the center.

❷ Use a fork to beat the eggs lightly in a small bowl. Pour the beaten eggs into the hollow center of the mound of flour and cocoa powder.

❶ Use a fork or your fingertips to gradually incorporate the eggs into the flour. Take care not to break the wall of flour or the eggs will run. When the flour and cocoa have all been absorbed gather the dough up into a ball.

❷ Wash and dry your hands and begin the kneading process. Place the dough on a clean work surface. At first it will be rough and grainy.

❸ After 20 minutes the dough should be smooth and silky, with tiny air bubbles visible on the surface. Wrap the dough in plastic wrap (cling film) and let rest for 30 minutes.

Colored pasta

Colored fresh pasta can be made by adding concentrated purées of tomato, bell pepper (capsicum), spinach, Swiss chard, carrot, or beet (beetroot). You can also make striking black pasta using squid's ink. As with aromatic pasta, the coloring agent will add extra flavor; be sure that your sauce does not clash with or override this flavor.

Preparing the colorant

For tomato pasta use ready-made tomato paste. For spinach, Swiss chard, bell pepper, carrot, or beet root pasta, cook the vegetable in lightly salted water until just tender then chop in a food processor until smooth.

Tomato pasta

Ingredients

- 2$\frac{1}{3}$ cups/350 g all-purpose/plain flour
- $\frac{1}{3}$ cup/50 g tomato purée or paste
- 3 very fresh large eggs

Sift the flour onto a clean work surface (preferably made of wood) and shape into a mound. Make a hollow in the center.

❷

Use a fork to beat the eggs lightly in a small bowl. Add the tomato paste to the eggs and pour them into the hollow center of the mound of flour.

Use a fork or your fingertips to gradually incorporate the eggs into the flour. Take care not to break the wall of flour or the eggs will run. When the flour has all been absorbed gather the dough up into a ball.

❷

Wash and dry your hands and begin the kneading process. Place the dough on a clean work surface. At first it will be rough and grainy.

❸

After 20 minutes the dough should be smooth and silky, with tiny air bubbles visible on the surface. Wrap the dough in plastic wrap (cling film) and let rest for 30 minutes.

Simple Fresh

The recipes in this chapter include all the classic ribbon shapes, from slender tagliolini and taglierini, to medium-sized tagliatelle (fettuccine) and the widest pappardelle. There are also recipes for maltagliati (badly cut!) and stracci (rags). Combining the sauce with the right pasta shape is an art that we have worked to refine and perfect over many years of teaching. We have included a wide variety of dishes, from the unusual *Chestnut tagliatelle with Ricotta cheese* and *Coffee tagliatelle with quails* to the more traditional, such as *Saffron pappardelle with lamb sauce.*

Above: Cool taglierini (page 58)
Left: Spicy tagliatelle with creamy eggplant sauce (page 44)

FAZZOLETTI CON LA SALSICCIA
Pasta with Italian sausages

Pasta
- 1 quantity plain fresh pasta dough (see chart on page 8)
- 2 tablespoons coarse sea salt (to cook the pasta)

Sauce
- 3 fresh Italian sausages (about 10 oz/300 g)
- 2 tablespoons extra-virgin olive oil
- 1 red onion, finely chopped
- salt and freshly ground black pepper to taste
- 1 pinch ground cinnamon
- $^1/_2$ cup/125 ml dry red wine
- 1 cup/250 g canned tomatoes, coarsely chopped
- 4 tablespoons freshly grated Parmesan cheese

Prepare the pasta dough following the instructions on pages 9–11. • Roll the sheets of pasta one notch at a time down to the thinnest setting. Dry the sheets of pasta on a lightly floured cloth for 30 minutes. • Cut into strips about $^3/_4$ inch (2 cm) wide and then into triangles with 2-inch (5-cm) bases. • Place a large pan of water over high heat with the coarse sea salt. Cover and bring to a boil. • Sauce: Prick the sausages well with the tines (prongs) of a fork and cook for 3 minutes in a pan of boiling water. Drain, peel, and chop them coarsely. • Heat the oil in a large skillet (frying pan) over low heat and sweat the onion with a pinch of salt for 10 minutes. • Add the chopped sausage meat and sauté over high heat for 5 minutes. • Season with the cinnamon, salt, and pepper. Pour in the wine and cook until evaporated. • Add the tomatoes and cook for 20 minutes over low heat. • Cook the pasta in the pan of boiling water until al dente, about 4 minutes. • Drain the pasta and add to the skillet with the sauce. Toss gently and sprinkle with the Parmesan. • Serve immediately.

Serves 4; Preparation: 30 minutes + time to make the pasta; Cooking: 30 minutes; Level: 2

PAPPARDELLE ALLO ZAFFERANO IN SALSA DI AGNELLO
Saffron pappardelle with lamb sauce

Pasta
- $3^1/_3$ cups/500 g unbleached flour
- 4 very fresh large eggs + 2 very fresh large egg yolks
- 1 teaspoon ground saffron, dissolved in 1 tablespoon warm water
- pinch of ground saffron (for the cooking water)
- 2 tablespoons coarse sea salt (to cook the pasta)

Sauce
- 4 tablespoons extra-virgin olive oil
- 3 tablespoons butter
- 1 leg of lamb, weighing about $2^1/_2$ lb/1.2 kg
- $^1/_2$ cup/125 ml Vin Santo or sherry
- salt and freshly ground white pepper to taste
- 1 quart/1 liter meat stock (see page 97)
- 1 small onion, finely chopped
- 2 tablespoons all-purpose/plain flour
- 1 lettuce heart, cut in strips
- 1 tablespoon finely chopped marjoram
- 6–8 threads saffron, crumbled

Prepare the pasta dough following the instructions on pages 9–11, adding the saffron and water mixture to the eggs. Wrap the dough in plastic wrap (cling film) and let rest for 30 minutes. • Divide the dough into 6 pieces. Roll it through the machine one notch at a time down to the thinnest setting. • Use a knife to cut into pappardelle about 5 x $^3/_4$ inches (12 x 2 cm). Let dry on a lightly floured cloth for 30 minutes. • Sauce: Heat the oil and butter in a large casserole or saucepan over high heat and sauté the lamb until browned all over. • Pour in the wine or sherry and cook until evaporated. • Season with salt and pepper, lower the heat, and cook for 1 hour, or until very tender, moistening with enough stock to keep the sauce moist. • Take the lamb out of the pan and remove the meat from the bone. Cut the meat into small strips. • Add 3 tablespoons of stock to the pan with the cooking juices. Add the onion and cook for 5 minutes. • Add the lamb and cook for 3–5 minutes more. Stir in the flour and 2 cups (500 ml) of stock. Add the lettuce, marjoram, and saffron and season with salt and pepper. Cook over low heat until the lettuce has wilted and the sauce has thickened, about 5 minutes. • About 30 minutes before the sauce is ready, place a large pan of water over high heat with the coarse sea salt and pinch of powdered saffron. Cover and bring to a boil. • Cook the pappardelle until al dente, about 4–5 minutes. Drain well and transfer to a heated serving dish. Spoon the sauce over the top and toss gently. • Serve hot.

Serves 4; Preparation: 40 minutes + time to make the pasta; Cooking: 1 hour 30 minutes; Level: 3

MALTAGLIATI AI FAGIOLI
Pasta with beans

Pasta
- 2²/₃ cups/400 g durum wheat flour
- 4 tablespoons extra-virgin olive oil
- about ³/₄ cup/180 ml warm water
- 2 tablespoons coarse sea salt (to cook the pasta)

Sauce
- 5 tablespoons extra-virgin olive oil
- 2 cloves garlic, finely chopped
- 2 tablespoons finely chopped fresh herbs
  (rosemary, sage, thyme)
- 1 dried red chile pepper, crumbled
- 1 lb/500 g mixed cooked beans (cannellini, borlotti, azuki),
  drained
- 4 tomatoes, peeled, seeds removed, and cut in strips
- salt to taste
- 3 oz/90 g prosciutto/Parma ham, cut in julienne strips
  (matchsticks)
- 2 cups/500 ml water
- 5 tablespoons red wine vinegar
- 1 large red onion, sliced

Prepare the pasta dough following the instructions on pages 9–11, using the flour, oil, and enough water to obtain a fairly firm dough. Knead for 20 minutes, then wrap in plastic wrap (cling film) and let rest for 30 minutes. • Divide the dough in 4 pieces and roll each one through the machine one notch at a time down to the thinnest setting. Dry the sheets of pasta on a lightly floured cloth for 30 minutes. • Cut into irregularly-shaped pieces (see page 14). • Place a large pan of water over high heat with the coarse sea salt. Cover and bring to a boil. • Sauce: Heat 4 tablespoons of oil in a large skillet (frying pan) over high heat and sauté the garlic, herbs, and chile pepper for 1 minute. • Add the drained beans and cook for 5 minutes over medium heat. Add the tomatoes, season with salt, cover, and cook for 10 minutes. • Heat the remaining oil in a small skillet over high heat and sauté the prosciutto until the pieces of fat are transparent. Add to the bean sauce. • Bring the 2 cups (500 ml) of water to a boil with the vinegar and a pinch of salt and cook the onion in it for 2 minutes. Drain and set aside. • Cook the pasta in the pan of boiling water until al dente, about 4 minutes. • Drain the pasta and add to the skillet with the sauce. Toss gently, adding the onion and little of the cooking water if the sauce is too dry. • Serve hot.

Serves 4; Preparation: 30 minutes + time to make the pasta; Cooking: 30 minutes; Level: 2

TAGLIATELLE DI CASTAGNE ALLA RICOTTA
Chestnut tagliatelle with Ricotta cheese

Pasta
- 1 quantity chestnut pasta dough (see chart on page 8)
- 2 tablespoons coarse sea salt (to cook the pasta)

Sauce
- 1¹/₃ quarts/1.3 liters milk (of which 1 quart/1 liter will be used to cook the tagliatelle)
- 16 dried chestnuts
- 10 oz/300 g Ricotta cheese, strained
- ¹/₂ cup/125 ml fresh cream
- 1¹/₄ cups/150 g freshly grated Parmesan cheese
- salt and freshly ground white pepper to taste
- freshly grated nutmeg to taste

Prepare the chestnut tagliatelle following the instructions on pages 9–11. • Sauce: Heat 1¹/₄ cups (310 ml) of milk in a small saucepan and cook the chestnuts until tender, about 45 minutes–1 hour. Drain and chop them coarsely. • Place the remaining milk and enough water to fill a large pan over high heat with the coarse sea salt. Cover and bring to a boil. • Heat the Ricotta and cream in a large skillet (frying pan) over over low heat. Season with salt, pepper, and nutmeg and keep warm. • Cook the pasta in the pan of boiling milk and water until al dente, about 3 minutes. • Drain the pasta and add to the skillet with the Ricotta. Toss gently with the Parmesan and chestnuts. • Serve hot.

Serves 4; Preparation: 30 minutes + time to make the pasta; Cooking: 1 hour 15 minutes; Level: 2

TAGLIATELLE CON SALSA CRUDA
Tagliatelle with uncooked cherry tomato sauce

Pasta
- 1 quantity plain fresh pasta dough (see chart on page 8)
- 2 tablespoons coarse sea salt (to cook the pasta)

Sauce
- 4 tablespoons extra-virgin olive oil
- 4 anchovy fillets
- 12 oz/350 g cherry tomatoes
- 1 clove garlic, finely chopped
- 1 tablespoon each finely chopped parsley and basil
- 1 spicy red or green chile pepper (optional)
- 8 oz/250 g bocconcini (Mozzarella balls)
- salt and freshly ground black pepper to taste

Prepare the tagliatelle following the instructions on pages 9–11. • Place a large pan of water over high heat with the coarse sea salt. Cover and bring to a boil. • Sauce: Heat the oil in a small saucepan and add the anchovies. Mash with a fork until dissolved in the oil. Remove from the heat. • Cut the tomatoes in halves or quarters and combine in a bowl with the garlic, parsley, basil, and chile pepper, if using. • Cook the pasta in the pan of boiling water until al dente, about 3–4 minutes. • Drain the pasta and transfer to a serving bowl. Add the tomato mixture and bocconcini, then pour the flavored oil over the top. Season with salt and pepper. • Toss gently and serve immediately.

Serves 4; Preparation: 25 minutes + time to make the pasta; Cooking: 5 minutes; Level: 2

CARBONARA DI TAGLIATELLE E ASPARAGI
Tagliatelle with asparagus and egg

Pasta
- 1 quantity plain fresh pasta dough (see chart on page 8)
- 2 tablespoons coarse sea salt (to cook the pasta)

Sauce
- 1 lb/500 g tender asparagus spears
- 3 tablespoons extra-virgin olive oil
- 8 oz/250 g guanciale or pancetta, thickly sliced, then cut in thin strips
- salt and freshly ground white pepper to taste
- $3/4$ cup/180 ml meat (see page 97) or vegetable stock
- 3 large egg yolks
- 1 cup/125 g freshly grated Parmesan cheese
- sprig of fresh mint, torn

Prepare the tagliatelle following the instructions on pages 9–11. • Place a large pan of water over high heat with the coarse sea salt. Cover and bring to a boil. • Sauce: Clean the asparagus. Separate the lower part of the stalks from the tender tips and cut the stalks into thick rounds. • Heat the oil in a large skillet (frying pan) over medium-high heat and sauté the guanciale or pancetta for 5 minutes. • Add the asparagus stalks and sauté for 3–4 minutes. • Season with salt and pepper and pour in half the stock. Cook over medium heat for 5 minutes. • Add the asparagus tips and cook for 3–4 minutes more, or until tender. • Cook the pasta in the boiling water until al dente, about 3–4 minutes. • Drain well and add to the skillet with the asparagus. Increase the heat and add the egg yolks and remaining stock, gently tossing all the time so that no lumps form. • Sprinkle with the Parmesan and mint and season with pepper. • Serve immediately.

Serves 4; Preparation: 20 minutes + time to make the pasta; Cooking: 25 minutes; Level: 2

Tagliatelle with asparagus and egg

TAGLIOLINI IN SALSA DI LATTUGA
Tagliolini in lettuce sauce

Pasta
- 3^1/$_3$ cups/500 g unbleached flour
- 5 very fresh large eggs
- 2 tablespoons coarse sea salt (to cook the pasta)

Sauce
- 1^1/$_2$ tablespoons butter
- 6 tablespoons extra-virgin olive oil
- 1 leek, cut in thin rings
- 1 small head lettuce, coarsely chopped
- 1 bunch green radicchio, coarsely chopped
- salt and freshly ground white pepper to taste
- about ^{1}/$_2$ cup/125 ml stock
- 3 shallots, sliced

Prepare the pasta dough using the flour and eggs following the instructions on pages 9–11. Wrap the dough in plastic wrap (cling film) and let rest for 30 minutes. • Divide the dough into 8 pieces and roll through the machine one notch at a time down to the thinnest setting. Cut the tagliolini into noodles about 2 mm wide. Shape into nests and dry on a lightly floured cloth for 30 minutes. • Place a large pan of water over high heat with the coarse sea salt. Cover and bring to a boil. • Sauce: Melt the butter and 2 tablespoons of oil in a medium saucepan over medium heat and sauté the leek for about 10 minutes until softened. • Gradually stir in the lettuce and radicchio. Season with salt and pepper and pour in the stock. Cover and cook over low heat for 15 minutes. • Remove from the heat and chop in a food processor. • Heat the remaining oil in a large skillet (frying pan) over high heat and fry the shallots until well browned. Drain on paper towels. • Heat the lettuce purée in a large skillet. • Cook the pasta in the pan of boiling water until al dente, about 1–2 minutes. • Drain the pasta and add to the skillet with the lettuce purée, adding 1–2 tablespoons of cooking water. Toss gently, then place the pasta in 4 individual serving dishes and garnish with the shallots. Serve immediately.

Serves 4; Preparation: 30 minutes + time to prepare the pasta; Cooking: 30 minutes; Level: 2

TAGLIATELLE AL CAFFÈ CON LE QUAGLIE
Coffee tagliatelle with quails

Pasta
- 1 quantity aromatic (coffee) pasta dough (see chart on page 8)
- 2 tablespoons coarse sea salt (to cook the pasta)

Sauce
- 1 tablespoon extra-virgin olive oil
- 1 heaping tablespoon butter
- 1 bouquet garni (a bunch of fresh sage, laurel, and thyme)
- 2 quails (about 1 lb/500 g), cleaned and ready to cook
- 3 tablespoons dry white wine
- 1 cup/250 ml meat stock (see page 97)
- ^{1}/$_2$ cup/125 ml dry Marsala wine
- 1 tablespoon very strong black coffee
- ^{3}/$_4$ cup/90 g freshly grated Pecorino romano cheese
- salt and freshly ground white pepper to taste

Prepare the tagliatelle following the instructions on pages 9–11, and 16. • Heat the oil and butter in a large casserole or skillet (frying pan) and sauté the bouquet garni briefly. • Add the quails and sauté over high heat until nicely browned all over, about 5 minutes. • Drizzle with the white wine and cook until evaporated. • Pour in 1 cup (250 ml) of stock. Cover and cook over low heat for about 20 minutes, or until the quail are tender and well cooked. • Place a large pan of water over high heat with the coarse sea salt. Cover and bring to a boil. • Remove the quails from the heat and let cool a little. Remove the skin and bone the quails, cutting the flesh into strips. Moisten the meat with a little stock and place in a warm oven. • Return the casserole with the cooking juices to the heat and drizzle with the Marsala, followed by the coffee. Strain the sauce and transfer it to a skillet large enough to hold the pasta. • Cook the pasta in the boiling water until al dente, about 3–4 minutes. • Drain well and add to the skillet with the sauce. Add the quail meat and toss gently. Sprinkle with the Pecorino and serve hot.

Serves 4; Preparation: 45 minutes + time to make the pasta; Cooking: 45 minutes; Level: 2

Above: Tagliolini in lettuce sauce

Below: Coffee tagliatelle with quails

PAPPARDELLE SUL FAGIANO
Pappardelle with pheasant

The pappardelle noodles in this recipe are thicker and larger than usual. When rolling the pasta through the machine, begin at the thickest setting and roll one notch at a time down to the second thinnest setting. Cut in noodles measuring about 1 x 8 inches (2.5 x 20 cm)

Sauce
- 14 oz/400 g cleaned pheasant, cut in small pieces
- 1 red onion, coarsely chopped
- 1 carrot, coarsely chopped
- 3 shallots, coarsely chopped
- 1 sprig rosemary
- 1 sprig sage
- 1 small piece of cinnamon stick
- 3 juniper berries, crushed
- 1 bay leaf
- 2 cloves
- 1 teaspoon whole black peppercorns
- 2 cups/500 ml dry red wine
- 2 cups/500 ml chicken stock
- 7 oz/200 g pitted/stoned dates, finely chopped
- salt to taste
- 4 tablespoons extra-virgin olive oil

Pasta
- 1 quantity plain fresh pasta dough (see chart on page 8)
- 2 tablespoons coarse sea salt (to cook the pasta)

Place the pheasant in an earthenware or ceramic dish and cover with the onion, carrot, shallots, rosemary, sage, cinnamon, juniper berries, bay leaf, cloves, and peppercorns. Pour in the wine, cover, and leave to marinate in the refrigerator overnight. • Prepare the pappardelle following the instructions on pages 9–11. • Drain the pheasant, reserving the marinade, and pat dry with paper towels. • Heat the oil in an earthenware casserole and sauté the pheasant over high heat for 10 minutes, stirring often. • Add the wine from the marinade and cook for 30 minutes, uncovered, over high heat. • Add the vegetables and spices from the marinade and season with salt. Cover and cook over low heat for 1 hour, or until the pheasant is tender, adding stock as needed to keep the sauce moist. • Place a large pan of water over high heat with the coarse sea salt. Cover and bring to a boil. • Chop the sauce in a food processor and return to the casserole. Add the dates and cook for another 15 minutes. • Cook the pasta in the pan of boiling water until al dente, about 5 minutes. • Drain the pasta and add to the casserole with the sauce. Toss gently and transfer to a heated serving dish. • Serve hot.

Serves 4; Preparation: 1 hour + time to marinate the pheasant + time to make the pasta; Cooking: 2 hours; Level: 2

LAGANE BIANCHE CON PASSATA DI CECI
Tagliatelle with garbanzo bean purée and red mullet

Sauce
- 7 oz/200 g dried garbanzo beans/chickpeas, soaked in salted water for 24 hours
- 1 bay leaf, torn in half
- 3 cloves garlic, 1 whole and 2 thinly sliced
- 6 tablespoons extra-virgin olive oil
- 2 small red chile peppers, cut in thin strips
- 14 oz/400 g red mullet fillets, cut in small chunks
- salt to taste

Pasta
- 1 1/3 cups/200 g durum wheat flour
- about 1/2 cup/125 ml water
- 2 tablespoons coarse sea salt (to cook the pasta)

Drain the garbanzo beans and place them in a large pan with the bay leaf, and the whole clove of garlic. Cover with plenty of cold water and cook for about 2 hours, or until tender. Season with salt just before they are cooked. • Prepare the tagliatelle dough using the flour and water following the instructions on pages 9–11. Let rest for 30 minutes, then roll the dough through the machine one notch at a time down to the thinnest setting. Cut into pieces about 3/4 x 3 inches (2 x 7 cm). Let dry on a lightly floured cloth for 30 minutes. • Place a large pan of water over high heat with the coarse sea salt. Cover and bring to a boil. • Drain the garbanzo beans when cooked, reserving the cooking water. • Chop the garbanzo beans in a food processor until smooth. Add enough of the reserved cooking water to obtain a soft purée. • Heat the oil in a large skillet (frying pan) over high heat and sauté the remaining sliced garlic, chile pepper, and red mullet for 2 minutes. Season with salt and remove from the heat. • Cook the pasta in the pan of boiling water until al dente, about 6–7 minutes. • Drain the pasta and place in a heated serving dish. • Reheat the garbanzo bean purée and toss gently with the pasta. • Spoon the red mullet sauce over the top and serve at once.

Serves 4; Preparation: 1 hour + 24 hours to soak garbanzo beans + time to prepare the pasta; Cooking: 3 hours; Level: 2

Tagliatelle with garbanzo bean purée and red mullet

PAPPARDELLE AL CONIGLIO
Pappardelle with rabbit sauce

The pappardelle noodles in this recipe are even thicker and larger than usual. When rolling the pasta through the machine, begin at the thickest setting and roll one notch at a time down to the third thinnest setting. Cut in noodles measuring about 1 x 10 inches (2.5 x 25 cm)

Pasta
- 1¼ quantities plain fresh pasta dough (see chart on page 8)
- 2 tablespoons coarse sea salt (to cook the pasta)

Sauce
- 4 tablespoons extra-virgin olive oil
- 1 medium red onion, finely chopped
- 1 medium carrot, finely chopped
- salt and freshly ground black pepper to taste
- 2 cloves garlic, finely chopped
- 1 tablespoon finely chopped parsley
- 1 sprig thyme
- 1 sprig sage
- 1 bay leaf
- 1 sprig rosemary
- 1 medium rabbit, about 2½ lb/1.2 kg, including the heart and liver, rabbit boned and cut in small pieces, heart and liver finely chopped
- ½ cup/125 ml dry white wine
- 1²/₃ cups/400 g peeled and chopped tomatoes
- 1 cup/250 ml meat stock (see page 97)
- ³/₄ cup/90 g freshly grated Parmesan cheese

Prepare the pappardelle following the instructions on pages 9–11. • Sauce: Heat the oil in an earthenware casserole and add the onion, carrot, and a pinch of salt. Cover and cook over low heat for 15 minutes. • Add the garlic, parsley, thyme, sage, bay leaf, and rosemary and cook over high heat for 5 minutes. • Add the rabbit, with the heart and liver, and sauté over high heat until well browned. • Pour in the wine and cook until evaporated. • Add the tomatoes and stock and season with salt and pepper. Partially cover the pan and simmer over low heat for about 1 hour, or until the meat is well cooked and the sauce is dense and creamy. • About 20 minutes before the sauce is ready, place a large pan of water over high heat with the coarse sea salt. Cover and bring to a boil. • Cook the pasta in the pan of boiling water until al dente, about 6 minutes. • Drain the pasta and add to the casserole with the sauce. Toss gently, adding the Parmesan. • Serve hot.

Serves 4; Preparation: 1 hour + time to make the pasta; Cooking: 2 hours; Level: 3

LAGANE ALLA GALLINELLA
Pasta with tomato and fish sauce

Pasta
- 2²/₃ cups/400 g durum wheat flour
- 2 very fresh large eggs
- about ½ cup/125 ml water
- 2 tablespoons coarse sea salt (to cook the pasta)

Sauce
- 1 cup/250 ml boiling fish stock (see page 97)
- 1 lb/500 g gurnard or other tasty, white-fleshed fish, cleaned and ready to cook
- 4 tablespoons extra-virgin olive oil
- 2 cloves garlic, finely chopped
- 1 dried chile pepper, crumbled
- 4 tablespoons dry white wine
- 4 tomatoes (about 8 oz/250 g), peeled and seeds removed
- salt to taste
- 1 tablespoon finely chopped parsley

Prepare the pasta dough following the instructions on pages 9–11, using the flour, eggs, and enough water to obtain a fairly firm dough. Knead for 10 minutes, then wrap in plastic wrap (cling film) and let rest for 30 minutes. • Divide the dough into 4–5 pieces. Roll them through the machine one notch at a time down to the second thinnest setting. • Dry the sheets of pasta on a lightly floured cloth for 30 minutes. • Cut into irregularly-shaped pieces about 2 x 2½ inches (4 x 6 cm). • Place a large pan of water over high heat with the coarse sea salt. Cover and bring to a boil. • Sauce: Place the fish stock in a pan large enough to hold the fish. Add the fish and cook over low heat for 10 minutes. • Remove from the heat and fillet the fish. Discard all the bones and crumble the flesh. Strain the cooking water and reserve. • Heat the oil in a large skillet (frying pan) over high heat and sauté the garlic and chile pepper for 1 minute. • Pour in the wine and cook until evaporated. • Add the fish and tomatoes and cook over high heat for 2–3 minutes without stirring, but shaking the pan frequently. Season with salt. Remove from the heat and stir in the parsley. • Cook the pasta in the pan of boiling water until al dente, about 4 minutes. • Drain the pasta and add to the skillet with the sauce. Toss gently and serve.

Serves 4; Preparation: 1 hour + time to make the pasta; Cooking: 40 minutes; Level: 2

QUADROTTI DI PASTA AL LATTE CON POMODORI GRATINATI

Milk pasta with cherry tomatoes

Pasta
- 1$^1/_3$ cups/200 g unbleached flour
- 1$^1/_3$ cups/200 g durum wheat flour
- 1 tablespoon extra-virgin olive oil
- about $^3/_4$ cup/180 ml warm milk
- 2 tablespoons coarse sea salt (to cook the pasta)

Sauce
- 1$^1/_2$ lb/750 g cherry tomatoes
- 4 tablespoons fine dry bread crumbs
- 3 cloves garlic, finely chopped
- 2 tablespoons finely chopped parsley
- 1 tablespoon finely chopped oregano
- 8 leaves fresh basil, torn
- pinch of sugar
- 6 tablespoons extra-virgin olive oil
- salt and freshly ground black pepper to taste

Prepare the pasta dough following the instructions on pages 9–11, using both flours, oil, and enough milk to obtain a fairly firm dough. Knead for 15 minutes, then wrap in plastic wrap (cling film) and let rest for 30 minutes. • Divide the dough in 4 pieces and roll them through the machine one notch at a time down to the second thinnest setting. Cut into 1-inch (3-cm) squares. Dry the sheets of pasta on a lightly floured cloth for 30 minutes. • Sauce: Preheat the oven to 350°F/180°C/gas 4. • Cut the cherry tomatoes in half. • Mix the bread crumbs, garlic, parsley, oregano, and half the basil in a small bowl. Add the sugar and half the oil. • Place the tomatoes in a large, shallow baking dish, cut-side up. Sprinkle with salt and the herb mixture and bake in the oven for 40 minutes. • Place a large pan of water over high heat with the coarse sea salt. Cover and bring to a boil. Cook the pasta in the pan of boiling water until al dente, about 4–5 minutes. • Drain the pasta and place in a heated serving dish. Spoon the tomatoes and their cooking liquid over the top. Drizzle with the remaining oil and sprinkle with the remaining basil and a generous grinding of pepper. Toss gently. • Serve hot.

Serves 4; Preparation: 30 minutes + time to make the pasta; Cooking: 45 minutes; Level: 2

TAGLIATELLE AL PETTO D'ANATRA E VERDURE

Tagliatelle with duck and vegetables

Pasta
- 1 quantity plain fresh pasta dough (see chart on page 8)
- 2 tablespoons coarse sea salt (to cook the pasta)

Sauce
- 2 small carrots, cut in julienne strips (matchsticks)
- white part of 1 leek, cut in julienne strips (matchsticks)
- 2 stalks celery, cut in julienne strips (matchsticks)
- 2 baby onions, sliced
- 4 tablespoons extra-virgin olive oil
- 1 shallot, finely chopped
- 1-inch/2.5-cm piece fresh ginger root, peeled and finely chopped
- 1 duck's breast, cut in thin strips
- $^1/_2$ cup/125 ml Vin Santo or sherry
- 6 champignon mushrooms, sliced
- 1 bunch Swiss chard, stalks removed and cut in thin strips
- 2 cups/500 ml chicken or vegetable stock
- 1 tablespoon cornstarch/cornflour
- 2 tablespoons all-purpose/plain flour
- 3 tablespoons butter, clarified if available
- salt and freshly ground black pepper to taste
- 2 tablespoons finely chopped parsley

Prepare the tagliatelle following the instructions on pages 9–11. Shape the tagliatelle into hanks or nests. • Sauce: Bring a large pan of salted water to a boil and blanch the carrots for 2 minutes. Drain and cool in a bowl of cold water and ice. Separately blanch and cool the leek, celery, and onions in the same way. • Place a large pan of water over high heat with the coarse sea salt. Cover and bring to a boil. • Heat the oil in a large skillet (frying pan) over medium heat and sauté the shallot for 4 minutes. Add the ginger. Pour in the wine or sherry and cook until evaporated. • Gradually add the mushrooms over high heat. Cook for 5 minutes, then stir in the blanched vegetables. Cook for 3 minutes more, then stir in the Swiss chard and half the stock. Cook over high heat for 2 minutes. • Lightly flour the pieces of duck. • Melt the butter in a large skillet over high heat and sauté the duck for 1 minute. Season with salt and pepper. Pour in the remaining wine and cook until evaporated. • Add the duck to the vegetables. • Stir the cornstarch into the remaining stock in a small bowl and pour into the skillet. Bring the sauce to a boil, then turn off the heat.• Meanwhile, cook the pasta in the boiling water until al dente, about 4–5 minutes. • Drain the pasta and place in the skillet with the sauce. Toss gently for 1 minute, adding a little cooking water if needed. Sprinkle with the parsley. • Serve hot.

Serves 6; Preparation: 1 hour + time to make the pasta; Cooking: 45 minutes; Level: 2

PAGLIA E FIENO AL GORGONZOLA
Mixed tagliatelle with Gorgonzola cheese

Pasta
- $^1/_2$ quantity plain fresh pasta dough (see chart on page 8)
- $^1/_2$ quantity colored (spinach) pasta dough (see chart on page 8)
- 2 tablespoons coarse sea salt (to cook the pasta)

Sauce
- 4 tablespoons butter, cut up
- 8 oz/250 g Gorgonzola dolce cheese, cut into small cubes
- $^2/_3$ cup/150 ml fresh cream
- salt and freshly ground white pepper to taste
- 4 tablespoons freshly grated Parmesan cheese (optional)

Prepare the tagliatelle pasta following the instructions on pages 9–11. • Place a large pan of water over high heat with the coarse sea salt. Cover and bring to a boil. • Sauce: Melt the butter in a medium saucepan over low heat and add the Gorgonzola and cream. Season with salt and pepper. Cook over low heat, stirring constantly, until the cheese has melted. • Cook the pasta in the pan of boiling water until al dente, about 2–3 minutes. • Drain the pasta and transfer to a heated serving dish. Add the Gorgonzola sauce, mixing carefully with two forks. • Sprinkle with the Parmesan, if liked.

Serves 4; Preparation: 20 minutes + time to prepare the pasta; Cooking: 10 minutes; Level: 2

MALFATTI DI MAIS AI FAGIOLI E SALSICCIA
Cornmeal pasta with cannellini beans and Italian sausages

Be sure to use Italian sausages in this recipe. The northern European, wurstel-type sausage will not work well.

Sauce
- 7 oz/200 g dried cannellini beans, soaked in cold water for 12 hours
- 4 tablespoons extra-virgin olive oil
- 2 sprigs fresh rosemary, 1 whole and 1 with leaves finely chopped
- salt and freshly ground black pepper to taste
- 14 oz/400 g very fresh Italian sausages (about 4 sausages)
- $^1/_2$ cup/125 ml dry white wine

Pasta
- 1 cup/150 g finely ground yellow cornmeal
- $1^2/_3$ cups/250 g unbleached flour
- 4 very fresh large eggs
- about 2 tablespoons warm water
- 2 tablespoons coarse sea salt (to cook the pasta)

Sauce: Drain the beans and place them in a large saucepan with 2 tablespoons of oil and the whole sprig of rosemary. Cover with plenty of cold water and cook for about 2 hours, or until tender. Season with salt just before they are cooked. • Prepare the pasta using the flour and water following the instructions on pages 9–11, and 14. Wrap the dough in plastic wrap (cling film) and let rest for 30 minutes. • Divide the dough into 4 pieces and roll them through the machine one notch at a time down to the thinnest setting. • Use a fluted pastry cutter to cut into diamond shapes, about $^3/_4$ x 2 inches (2 x 5 cm). Let dry on a lightly floured cloth for 30 minutes. • Place a large pan of water over high heat with the coarse sea salt. Cover and bring to a boil. • Drain the beans when cooked, discarding the rosemary and reserving the cooking water. • Chop the beans in a food processor until smooth. Add enough of the reserved cooking water to obtain a soft purée. • Prick the sausages with the tines (prongs) of a fork and cook in a pan of boiling water for 3 minutes. Remove the skins and break the sausages up using a fork. • Heat the remaining oil in a large skillet (frying pan) over high heat and sauté the sausages for 5 minutes. • Add the chopped rosemary and drizzle with the wine. Remove from the heat. • Cook the pasta in the pan of boiling water until al dente, about 5–6 minutes. • Drain the pasta and place in a heated serving dish. • Reheat the bean purée and toss gently with the pasta and sausage. • Serve hot.

Serves 4; Preparation: 2 hours + 12 hours to soak the beans + time to prepare the pasta; Cooking: 2 hours 30 minutes; Level: 2

Cornmeal pasta with cannellini beans and Italian sausages

QUADRETTI DI GRANO DURO AI CALAMARI
Durum wheat squares with squid

Pasta
- 1 quantity durum wheat pasta dough (see chart on page 8)
- 2 tablespoons coarse sea salt (to cook the pasta)

Sauce
- $1/2$ cup/125 ml extra-virgin olive oil
- 14 oz/400 g of small squid, skinned, bodies cut in thin rings (the tentacles can be frozen for use in other dishes)
- 1 large tomato (about $3^1/2$ oz/100 g), cut in small pieces
- 1 tablespoon finely chopped chervil
- 1 tablespoon finely chopped marjoram
- 1 tablespoon finely chopped thyme
- $3/4$ cup/180 ml boiling fish stock (see page 97)
- salt and freshly ground white pepper to taste

Prepare the pasta dough following the instructions on pages 9–11. • Rest for 30 minutes, then roll to $1/8$ inch (2 mm) thick and cut in 1-inch (2.5-cm) squares. Dry on a lightly floured work surface for 30 minutes • Place a large pan of water over high heat with the coarse sea salt. Cover and bring to a boil. • Cook the pasta in the pan of boiling water until very al dente, about 5–6 minutes. • Sauce: While the pasta is cooking, heat the oil in a large skillet (frying pan) over high heat and sauté the squid, tomato, chervil, marjoram, and thyme for 3 minutes. • Pour in the fish stock. Season with salt and pepper and cook until the sauce has reduced by half, about 2–3 minutes. • Serve immediately.

Serves 4; Preparation: 2 hours + time to prepare the pasta + time to make the fish stock; Cooking: 20 minutes; Level: 2

TAGLIATELLE AROMATICHE
Basil tagliatelle with vegetables

Pasta
- 1 quantity aromatic (basil) pasta dough (see chart on page 8)
- 2 tablespoons coarse sea salt (to cook the pasta)

Sauce
- 2 tablespoons butter
- 2 zucchini/courgettes, cut in julienne strips (matchsticks)
- 2 carrots, cut in julienne strips (matchsticks)
- 2 shallots, cut in julienne strips (matchsticks)
- $1/2$ cup/125 ml dry white wine
- $1/2$ cup/125 ml fresh cream
- $1/2$ cup/125 ml vegetable stock
- salt and freshly ground white pepper to taste
- freshly grated Parmesan cheese, to serve (optional)

Prepare the tagliatelle following the instructions on pages 9–11. • Place a large pan of water over high heat with the coarse sea salt. Cover and bring to a boil. • Sauce: Heat the butter in a large skillet (frying pan) over high heat and sauté the zucchini, carrots, and shallots for 3 minutes. • Pour with the wine and cook until evaporated. • Add the cream and stock. Cook for about 5 minutes until the vegetables are tender-crunchy, and the sauce has thickened slightly. Season with salt and pepper. • About 3–4 minutes before the sauce is ready, add the pasta to the pan of boiling water and cook until al dente. • Drain the pasta and add to the skillet with the sauce. Toss gently, and remove from the heat. • Sprinkle with the Parmesan, if liked, and serve hot.

Serves 4; Preparation: 40 minutes + time to prepare the pasta; Cooking: 20 minutes; Level: 2

Above: Durum wheat squares with squid

Below: Basil tagliatelle with vegetables

TAGLIOLINI CON PESTO DI MANDORLE, BASILICO E POMODORO

Tagliolini with almonds, basil, and tomato

Pasta
- 1 quantity plain fresh pasta dough (see chart on page 8)
- 2 tablespoons coarse sea salt (to cook the pasta)

Sauce
- 4 oz/125 g peeled almonds, finely chopped
- 1 clove garlic, finely chopped
- salt to taste
- 1 small bunch fresh basil
- 1 large ripe tomato, peeled, seeds removed, and chopped
- $1/2$ teaspoon red pepper flakes
- 3 tablespoons extra-virgin olive oil

Prepare the tagliolini following the instructions on pages 9–11. • Place a large pan of water over high heat with the coarse sea salt. Cover and bring to a boil. • Sauce: Chop the almonds, garlic, and a pinch of salt in a food processor until almost smooth. • Add the basil and tomato and chop until smooth. Season with salt, red pepper flakes, and the oil. Transfer to a serving dish. • Cook the pasta in the pan of boiling water until al dente, about 2–3 minutes. • Drain the pasta and place in the serving dish with the sauce, adding a little of the pasta water if the sauce is too dry. • Toss gently and serve hot.

Serves 4; Preparation: 15 minutes + time to make the pasta; Cooking: 2–3 minutes; Level: 2

MALTAGLIATI ZUCCHINE E VONGOLE

Pasta with zucchini and clams

The special "kneading" of the clams in this recipe is a secret from the old southern Italian city of Naples. Move the shellfish around in the bowl using the same kneading gesture you would use to prepare bread dough. This will release all the sand and dirt the clams contain. This method should only be used with clams; don't try it with mussels.

Pasta
- 1 quantity plain fresh pasta dough (see chart on page 8)
- 2 tablespoons coarse sea salt (to cook the pasta) + extra to soak the clams

Sauce
- 2 lb/1 kg clams, in shell
- $1/2$ cup/125 ml dry white wine
- 5 tablespoons extra-virgin olive oil
- 12 oz/350 g zucchini/courgettes, cut in wheels
- pinch of sugar
- salt to taste
- 4 sprigs fresh mint, finely chopped + a few leaves to garnish

Prepare the maltagliati pasta following the instructions on pages 9–11, and 14. • Sauce: Soak the clams in a large bowl of water with coarse sea salt (15 g for each liter of water) for 1 hour. • Drain the clams and knead them as you would bread for 10 minutes. Discard any that are open or broken. • Place a large pan of water over high heat with the coarse sea salt. Cover and bring to a boil. • Heat half the wine in a large skillet (frying pan) with half the clams. Cover and cook over medium heat until the clams are open. Check the clams often; they should not be allowed to cook for too long. Repeat with the remaining wine and clams. Discard any clams that have not opened. • Strain the cooking liquid and reserve. • Heat the oil in a large skillet over high heat and sauté the zucchini for 5 minutes. • Add the sugar, clams, and 3–4 tablespoons of cooking liquid. Season with salt and add the mint. Cook for 2–3 minutes, then turn off heat. • Meanwhile, cook the pasta in the pan of boiling water until al dente, about 4–5 minutes. • Drain the pasta and add to the skillet with the clam sauce. Toss gently over medium heat, adding a little more cooking liquid, if necessary. • Garnish with the mint leaves and serve hot in individual bowls.

Serves 4; Preparation: 30 minutes + 1 hour to soak clams + time to prepare the pasta; Cooking: 25 minutes; Level: 2

Pasta with zucchini and clams

TAGLIERINI AI MIRTILLI CON POMODORO E MOZZARELLA

Whortleberry taglierini with tomato and Mozzarella cheese

Choose top quality water buffalo Mozzarella for this dish. It should be very fresh and delicate in flavor.

Sauce
- 1¼ lb/625 g ripe tomatoes, peeled, seeded, and cut in ½-inch/1-cm cubes
- 4 tablespoons extra-virgin olive oil
- salt and freshly ground black pepper to taste
- 1 tablespoon fresh lemon juice
- 1 tablespoon sugar
- 8 leaves fresh mint, torn
- 7 oz/200 g Mozzarella cheese, cut in ½-inch/1-cm cubes

Pasta
- 2⅔ cups/400 g durum wheat flour
- 10 oz/300 g whortleberries or bilberries, chopped in a food processor and strained
- 2 tablespoons coarse sea salt (to cook the pasta)

Sauce: Place the tomatoes in a glass or ceramic bowl with the oil, salt, pepper, lemon juice, sugar, and mint. Refrigerate for 2 hours, stirring often. • Prepare the pasta dough following the instructions on pages 9–11, using the flour and whortleberry juice to obtain a fairly firm dough. If there is not enough fruit juice, add a little water. Knead for 10 minutes, then wrap in plastic wrap (cling film) and let rest for 30 minutes. Divide the dough in 4 pieces and roll each one in the machine one notch at a time down to the second thinnest setting. Cut the pasta into taglierini ¼-inch (3–4 mm) wide and shape into nests. Dry the pasta on a lightly floured cloth for 30 minutes. • Place a large pan of water over high heat with the coarse sea salt. Cover and bring to a boil. • Cook the pasta in the pan of boiling water until al dente, about 2–3 minutes. • Drain the pasta and add to the bowl with the sauce. Toss gently and serve in individual serving bowls. Garnish with the Mozzarella. • Serve immediately.

Serves 4; Preparation: 30 minutes + time to make the pasta and chill the sauce; Cooking: 2–3 minutes; Level: 2

TAGLIERINI ALLE TRIGLIE

Taglierini with red mullet sauce

Sauce
- 10 oz/300 g dried cannellini beans, soaked for 12 hours in cold water
- ½ onion
- 1 small carrot
- 1 stalk celery
- 1 sprig rosemary
- 1 bay leaf
- 5 tablespoons extra-virgin olive oil
- salt and freshly ground white pepper to taste
- 12 red mullet fillets, cleaned and bones removed
- juice of 1 lemon
- 6 tablespoons fine dry bread crumbs
- ½ shallot, finely chopped
- 1 tablespoon finely chopped parsley
- 1 tablespoon finely chopped thyme
- 3 tablespoons butter
- 1 tomato, seeds removed and coarsely chopped
- 1 sprig fresh basil

Pasta
- 1 quantity plain fresh pasta dough (see chart on page 8)
- 2 tablespoons coarse sea salt (to cook the pasta)

Sauce: Drain the beans and place in a saucepan with enough water to cover. Add the onion, carrot, celery, rosemary, bay leaf, and 2 tablespoons of oil. Cook over low heat for 2 hours, or until tender. • Season with salt just 5 minutes before the beans are cooked. • Drain, reserving the cooking water, and chop in a food processor with a little of the cooking water to obtain a fairly liquid purée. • Prepare the taglierini following the instructions on pages 9–11. • Place the red mullet fillets in a glass bowl. Season with salt and pepper and drizzle with the lemon juice. Refrigerate for 1 hour. • Place a large pan of water over high heat with the coarse sea salt. Cover and bring to a boil. • Preheat the oven to 450°F/220°C/gas 7. • Butter an ovenproof dish. • Mix the bread crumbs, shallot, parsley, and thyme in a small bowl with salt and pepper. Dredge the red mullet fillets in the mixture and transfer to the baking dish. Sprinkle with the bread crumb mixture and bake in the oven until tender, about 10–15 minutes. • Cook the pasta in the pan of boiling water until al dente, about 3 minutes. • Heat the bean purée and spoon into 4 individual dishes. • Drain the pasta thoroughly, toss with the butter, then divide evenly among the bowls. Spoon the red mullet over the top and garnish with the tomato, basil, and remaining oil. • Serve hot.

Serves 4; Preparation: 1 hour + time to make the pasta; Cooking: 3 hours; Level: 3

TAGLIATELLE COL SALAME

Tagliatelle with salami

Pasta
- 1 quantity plain fresh pasta dough (see chart on page 8)
- 2 tablespoons coarse sea salt (to cook the pasta)

Sauce
- 4 tablespoons extra-virgin olive oil
- 1 large onion, cut in thin rings
- 5 oz/150 g Tuscan salami, thickly sliced and cut in strips
- 4 tablespoons dry white wine
- 1 lb/500 g tomatoes, peeled, seeded, and chopped
- salt to taste
- 3^{1}/$_2$ oz/100 g Provolone dolce cheese, cut in strips
- 1 tablespoon finely chopped parsley
- 4 tablespoons freshly grated Parmesan cheese

Prepare the tagliatelle following the instructions on pages 9–11. • Sauce: Heat the oil in a large skillet (frying pan) over medium heat and sauté the onion for 10 minutes. • Add the salami and cook for 30 seconds over high heat. • Pour in the wine and cook until evaporated. • Stir in the tomatoes. Season with salt, partially cover, and cook over low heat for 20 minutes. • Place a large pan of water over high heat with the coarse sea salt. Cover and bring to a boil. • Cook the pasta in the pan of boiling water until al dente, about 4–5 minutes. • While the pasta is cooking, add the Provolone cheese to the pan so that it melts slightly. • Drain the pasta and add to the skillet with the salami. Toss gently for 1 minute, then turn off heat. Sprinkle with the parsley and Parmesan. • Serve hot.

Serves 4; Preparation: 30 minutes + time to make the pasta; Cooking: 40 minutes; Level: 2

TAGLIERINI CON GAMBERI E SALSA D'AGLIO

Taglierini with shrimp and garlic sauce

Pasta
- 1 quantity mixed durum pasta dough (see chart on page 8)
- 2 tablespoons coarse sea salt (to cook the pasta)

Sauce
- 7 oz/200 g garlic, peeled
- ^{3}/$_4$ cup/200 ml milk
- ^{1}/$_2$ cup/125 ml extra-virgin olive oil
- 12 anchovy fillets
- 8 oz/250 g peeled, deveined shrimp, cut in half if large
- 1 tablespoon finely chopped parsley
- 8 leaves fresh basil, torn
- salt to taste

Prepare the taglierini following the instructions on pages 9–11. • Place a large pan of water over high heat with the coarse sea salt. Cover and bring to a boil. • Sauce: Place the garlic in a small saucepan with 4 tablespoons of milk. Bring to a boil and then strain, discarding the milk. Repeat twice more with the remaining milk and the same garlic. Discard the milk. • Place the garlic in a food processor with 6 tablespoons of oil and chop until smooth. • Place 1 tablespoon of water in a small saucepan over low heat and dissolve the anchovies. Add 3 tablespoons of oil, then chop in a food processor until smooth. • Heat 1 tablespoon of oil in a large skillet (frying pan) and sauté the shrimp over high heat for 3 minutes. Season with salt and keep warm. • Cook the pasta in the pan of boiling water until al dente, about 3 minutes. Drain the pasta and add to the pan with the shrimp and the garlic sauce. Toss gently and place in 4 individual serving bowls. Spoon the anchovy sauce over the top and garnish with the parsley and basil. • Serve immediately.

Serves 4; Preparation: 45 minutes + time to make the pasta; Cooking: 40 minutes; Level: 2

TAGLIATELLE ALLE ORTICHE E CAPRINO
Nettle tagliatelle with goat's cheese

Pasta
- 3 cups/450 g unbleached flour
- 4 very fresh large eggs
- $3^1/_2$ oz/100 g cooked nettles (about 10 oz/300 g uncooked weight)
- 2 tablespoons coarse sea salt (to cook the pasta)

Sauce
- 3 tablespoons extra-virgin olive oil
- $^1/_2$ onion, finely chopped
- 1 clove garlic, finely chopped
- 14 oz/400 g nettles (tender, young part only)
- salt and freshly ground white pepper to taste
- 4 oz/125 g fresh creamy goat's cheese
- 4 tablespoons fresh cream

Rinse all ($1^1/_2$ lb/750 g) of nettles under cold running water (be sure to wear gloves). Cook the nettles in a large pan of salted water for 4 minutes. Drain well, let cool, and chop finely with a knife. • Prepare the pasta dough following the instructions on pages 9–11, and 17, using the flour, eggs, and $3^1/_2$ oz (100 g) of the chopped nettles to obtain a fairly firm dough. Knead for 15 minutes, then wrap in plastic wrap (cling film) and let rest for 30 minutes. • Divide the dough in 6 pieces and roll each one through the machine one notch at a time down to the second thinnest setting. Dry the sheets of pasta on a lightly floured cloth for 30 minutes, then cut into tagliatelle. • Place a large pan of water over high heat with the coarse sea salt. Cover and bring to a boil. • Sauce: Heat the oil in a large skillet (frying pan) and cook the onion over low heat for 15 minutes, adding a little water if necessary. • Add the garlic and remaining cooked nettles and season with salt and pepper. Cook for 5 minutes. • Mash the goat's cheese with the cream in a small bowl with a fork. • Cook the pasta in the pan of boiling water until al dente, about 4–5 minutes. • Drain the pasta and add to the skillet with the sauce. Toss gently for 1 minute, adding a little cooking water to make the sauce creamy. Spoon the goat's cheese over the top and turn off heat. • Serve hot.

Serves 6: Preparation: 45 minutes + time to make the pasta; Cooking: 30 minutes; Level: 2

PAPPARDELLE NERE CON SCAMPI E ZUCCHINE
Black pappardelle with Dublin Bay prawns

Pasta
- 1 quantity black pasta dough (see chart on page 8)
- 2 tablespoons coarse sea salt (to cook the pasta)

Sauce
- 3 large cloves garlic, 2 whole, 1 lightly crushed
- $^3/_4$ cup/180 ml milk
- scant $^1/_2$ cup/100 ml extra-virgin olive oil
- 10 oz/300 g small zucchini/courgettes (only the peel will be used)
- 1 large bunch parsley
- 2 small bunches basil, tough stalks removed
- salt and freshly ground black pepper to taste
- 7 Dublin Bay prawns, 5 peeled and 2 cut in half, to garnish
- scant $^1/_2$ cup/100 ml dry white wine
- $^1/_2$ cup/100 ml boiling fish stock (see page 97)

Prepare the pappardelle following the instructions on pages 9–11. • Sauce: Place the 2 whole cloves of garlic in a small saucepan with 4 tablespoons of milk. Bring to a boil and then strain, discarding the milk. Repeat twice more with the remaining milk and the same garlic. Discard the milk. • Place the garlic in a food processor with 4 tablespoons of oil and chop until smooth. • Place a large pan of water over high heat with the coarse sea salt. Cover and bring to a boil. • Peel the zucchini with a potato peeler (the insides can be used for another dish). Blanch the zucchini peel in salted, boiling water for 2–3 minutes. Drain and cool in cold water. Drain well. • Trim the tough stems off the parsley and blanch in salted, boiling water for 1 minute. Drain and cool in cold water. Drain well. • Chop the zucchini peel, parsley, garlic mixture, basil, and 4 tablespoons of oil in a food processor until smooth. Season with salt and pepper. • Cut 4 of the peeled prawns in rounds and finely chop the remaining peeled prawn. • Heat 1 tablespoon of oil in a large skillet (frying pan) and sauté for 1–2 minutes. • Pour in the wine and cook until evaporated. Season with salt and pepper and remove from the heat. • Cook the pasta in the pan of boiling water until al dente, about 4 minutes. • While the pasta is cooking, heat 1 tablespoon of oil in a skillet and sauté the 4 remaining pieces of prawn with the crushed garlic for about 1 minute. Discard the garlic. • Drain the pasta and add to the pan with the prawns. Add the fish stock and toss gently. • Remove from the heat and add the parsley and basil sauce. • Serve hot in individual bowls, each one garnished with a piece of prawn.

Serves 4; Preparation: 3 hours + time to prepare the pasta + time to make the fish stock; Cooking: 40 minutes; Level: 2

Black pappardelle with Dublin Bay prawns

TAGLIATELLE ALLE CASTAGNE CON FUNGHI

Chestnut tagliatelle with porcini mushrooms

This dish is typical of the many wooded areas of central Italy, where porcini mushrooms grow wild in chestnut woods during warm, wet weather in spring and autumn. If you can't get porcini mushrooms, replace with the same quantity of other wild mushrooms.

Pasta
• 1 quantity chestnut pasta dough (see chart on page 8)
• 2 tablespoons coarse sea salt (to cook the pasta)

Sauce
• 2 tablespoons extra-virgin olive oil
• 2 cloves garlic, finely chopped
• 1 sprig rosemary
• 1 bay leaf
• 1/2 teaspoon fennel seeds
• 10 oz/300 g fresh porcini (or other wild mushrooms), cleaned and cut in cubes
• 2 tablespoons butter
• 3/4 cup/200 ml boiling meat stock (see page 97)
• salt and freshly ground black pepper to taste

Prepare the chestnut tagliatelle following the instructions on pages 9–11. • Place a large pan of water over high heat with the coarse sea salt. Cover and bring to a boil. • Sauce: Heat the oil in a large skillet (frying pan) and sauté the garlic, rosemary, bay leaf, and fennel seeds until the garlic is pale gold. • Add the mushrooms. Cover and cook over medium heat until tender, about 10 minutes (depending on the type of mushroom). Add a little hot stock or water if the mushrooms dry out too much during cooking. Season with salt. • Cook the pasta in the pan of boiling water until al dente, about 3 minutes. • Drain the pasta and add to the skillet with the mushrooms. Toss gently with the butter, adding 1–2 tablespoons of stock or cooking water, if needed. • Place in individual serving dishes and garnish each one with a generous grinding of black pepper. • Serve hot.

Serves 4; Preparation: 30 minutes + time to make the pasta; Cooking: 20 minutes; Level: 2

TAGLIATELLE AL ROSMARINO

Rosemary tagliatelle in lamb sauce

Pasta
• 1 quantity aromatic (rosemary) pasta dough (see chart on page 8)
• 2 tablespoons coarse sea salt (to cook the pasta)

Sauce
• 4 tablespoons extra-virgin olive oil
• 2 cloves garlic, finely chopped
• 1 sprig fresh rosemary
• 1 dried chile pepper, crumbled
• 10 oz/300 g boned lamb, cut in small cubes
• 4 tablespoons dry white wine
• 6 large tomatoes, peeled, seeded, and coarsely chopped, or 1-lb/450-g can tomato pieces
• salt and freshly ground black pepper to taste
• 1 tablespoon finely chopped parsley
• sprigs of fresh rosemary, to garnish

Prepare the rosemary tagliatelle following the instructions on pages 9–11, and 16. • Sauce: Heat the oil in a large skillet (frying pan) over high heat and sauté the garlic, rosemary, and chile pepper for 3 minutes. • Add the lamb and sauté until browned all over. • Drizzle with the wine and cook until evaporated. • Add the tomatoes and season with salt and pepper. Cover and cook over low heat for 30 minutes. • Place a large pan of water over high heat with the coarse sea salt. Cover and bring to a boil. • About 3–4 minutes before the sauce is ready, add the pasta to the pan of boiling water and cook until al dente. • Drain the pasta and place in the skillet with the sauce. Add the parsley, toss gently, and remove from the heat. • Garnish with the sprigs of rosemary and serve hot.

Serves 4; Preparation: 40 minutes + time to prepare the pasta; Cooking: 40 minutes; Level: 2

Above: Chestnut tagliatelle with porcini mushrooms

Below: Rosemary tagliatelle in lamb sauce

PICAGGE VERDI
Rustic tagliatelle

Sauce
- 4 tablespoons extra-virgin olive oil
- 1 large red onion, finely chopped
- 1 stalk celery, finely chopped
- 1 carrot, finely chopped
- 14 oz/400 g stew beef, cut into large chunks
- $1/2$ oz/15 g dried porcini mushrooms, soaked in warm water, drained, and finely chopped
- 1 tablespoon finely chopped fresh parsley
- 1 tablespoon all-purpose/plain flour
- $1/2$ cup/125 ml dry white wine
- 10 oz/300 g tomatoes, peeled, seeded, and coarsely chopped
- salt and freshly ground black pepper to taste
- water (optional)

Pasta
- $2^2/3$ cups/400 g all-purpose/plain flour
- 2 eggs
- 2 oz/60 g herbs (parsley, thyme, basil, mint, etc.), boiled, squeezed dry, and finely chopped
- 1 tablespoon crumbled Italian sausage meat
- 1 tablespoon freshly grated Parmesan cheese
- 4 tablespoons dry white wine + more as needed

Sauce: Heat the oil in a large skillet (frying pan) and sauté the onion, celery, and carrot over high heat for 5 minutes. • Add the beef and cook until browned all over. • Add the mushrooms and parsley and cook for 3 minutes. • Stir in the flour, letting it soak up the oil. • Pour in the wine and cook until evaporated. • Add the tomatoes and season with salt and pepper. Cover and simmer over low heat, stirring occasionally, for about 1 hour, or until the meat is tender, adding water if the sauce begins to dry. • Pasta: Sift the flour onto a work surface and make a well in the center. Use a wooden spoon to stir in the eggs, herbs, sausage meat, Parmesan, and enough wine to make a smooth dough. Shape the dough into a ball, wrap in plastic wrap (cling film), and let rest for 30 minutes. • Roll the dough through the machine one notch at a time down to the thinnest setting. Place on a clean cloth and let rest for 30 minutes. • Cut into $1/2$-inch (1-cm) wide strips. • Place a large pan of water over high heat with the coarse sea salt. Cover and bring to a boil. • Cook the pasta in the boiling water until al dente, about 4–5 minutes. • Drain and add to the skillet with the meat sauce. Serve hot.

Serves 6; Preparation: 1 hour + 1 hour to make the pasta; Cooking: 1 hour 10 minutes; Level: 2

PIZZOCCHERI ALLA ZUCCA
Buckwheat pasta with pumpkin

Pasta
- 2 cups/300 g buckwheat flour
- 1 cup/150 g unbleached flour
- pinch of salt
- $3/4$ cup/180 ml water
- 2 tablespoons coarse sea salt (to cook the pasta)

Sauce
- $1^1/2$ lb/750 g winter squash or pumpkin, cut in pieces but not peeled
- 3 tablespoons butter
- pinch of sugar
- salt to taste
- 5 oz/150 g creamy Gorgonzola cheese

Prepare the pasta dough following the instructions on pages 9–11, using both flours, the salt, and enough water to obtain a fairly firm dough. Knead for 20 minutes, then wrap in plastic wrap (cling film) and let rest for 30 minutes. • Divide the dough in 6 pieces and roll each one through the machine one notch at a time down to the third from thinnest setting. Dry the sheets of pasta on a lightly floured cloth for 30 minutes. • Cut into $1/2$ x 2-inch (1 x 5-cm) pieces. • Sauce: Preheat the oven to 400°F/200°C/gas 6. • Bake the pumpkin for about 40 minutes, or until tender. Cool a little, then remove the peel and cut the flesh into small dice. • Place a large pan of water over high heat with the coarse sea salt. Cover and bring to a boil. • Melt the butter in a casserole and sauté the pumpkin with the sugar for 2–3 minutes. Season with salt and remove from the heat. • Cook the pasta in the pan of boiling water until al dente, about 5 minutes. • While the pasta is cooking, melt the Gorgonzola in a heavy-bottomed pan with 1–2 tablespoons of cooking water from the pan. • Drain the pasta and add to the casserole with the sauce. Toss gently, adding the pieces of pumpkin. • Serve hot.

Serves 4; Preparation: 30 minutes + time to make the pasta; Cooking: 50 minutes; Level: 2

Buckwheat pasta with pumpkin

TAGLIATELLE CON SCAMPI E GAMBERONI
Tagliatelle with prawns and shrimp

Pasta
- 1 quantity plain fresh pasta dough (see chart on page 8)
- 2 tablespoons coarse sea salt (to cook the pasta)

Sauce
- 1 lb/500 g Dublin Bay prawns
- 14 oz/400 g shrimp
- salt and freshly ground white pepper to taste
- 4 tablespoons butter
- 1 clove garlic, whole but crushed with the blade of a knife
- 4 tablespoons dry white wine
- $^1/_2$ cup/125 ml fresh cream
- 1 tablespoon finely chopped tarragon
- 1 tablespoon finely chopped parsley

Prepare the tagliatelle following the instructions on pages 9–11. • Place a large pan of water over high heat with the coarse sea salt. Cover and bring to a boil. • Sauce: Peel the prawns and shrimp and devein them. Remove their heads (and reserve them). Cut the meat in small cubes. • Place the heads in a large saucepan with plenty of cold water, season with salt, and bring to a boil. Cook, uncovered, over medium heat for 30 minutes. Strain, discarding the heads and reserve the stock to cook the pasta. • Melt half the butter in a large skillet (frying pan) over medium heat and sauté the garlic, shrimp, and prawns for 2–3 minutes. • Pour in the wine and cook until evaporated. • Add the cream and tarragon and cook for 2 minutes. Discard the garlic. • Meanwhile, cook the pasta in the pan of boiling stock until al dente, about 4–5 minutes. • Drain the pasta and add to the skillet with the seafood. Add the remaining butter and 4 tablespoons of the stock in which the pasta was cooked. Toss gently for 1 minute, then turn off heat. Sprinkle with the tarragon and parsley. • Serve hot.

Serves 4; Preparation: 1 hour + time to make the pasta; Cooking: 50 minutes; Level: 2

TAGLIATELLE AL PEPERONCINO CON CREMA DI MELANZANE
Spicy tagliatelle with creamy eggplant sauce

Pasta
- $2^2/_3$ cups/400 g unbleached flour
- 4 very fresh large eggs
- 2 dried chile peppers, seeded and crumbled
- 1 teaspoon finely chopped fresh thyme
- 2 tablespoons coarse sea salt (to cook the pasta)

Sauce
- 3 medium, oval-shaped eggplants/aubergines
- 6 tablespoons extra-virgin olive oil
- 2 cloves garlic, finely chopped
- 1 sprig fresh thyme
- 15 leaves fresh basil, torn
- salt and freshly ground white pepper to taste
- 3 ripe tomatoes, peeled, seeded, and chopped
- 6 tablespoons freshly grated Pecorino romano cheese

Prepare the tagliatelle following the instructions on pages 9–11, adding the chile pepper and thyme to the egg yolks. • Sauce: Peel the eggplants and chop into 1 inch (2.5 cm) cubes. Boil in lightly salted water for 4 minutes. Drain, squeezing out the excess moisture. • Place a large pan of water over high heat with the coarse sea salt. Cover and bring to a boil. • Heat the oil in a large skillet (frying pan) and sauté the garlic and thyme for 2 minutes. • Add the eggplant and cook for 6–7 minutes, mashing gently with the back of a fork. • Remove from the heat, add half the basil, and season with salt and pepper. Let cool a little and then chop in a food processor until smooth. • Return the eggplant cream to the skillet and add the tomato. Cook until the tomatoes have broken down and the sauce is creamy. • Cook the pasta in the pan of boiling water until al dente, about 4–5 minutes. • Drain the pasta and add to the skillet with the sauce. Add 2–3 tablespoons of cooking water, sprinkle with the cheese and remaining basil, and toss gently. • Serve hot.

Serves 4; Preparation: 45 minutes + time to make the pasta; Cooking: 30 minutes; Level: 2

TAGLIATELLE IN SALSA D'UOVO
Tagliatelle with egg sauce

Pasta
- 1 quantity plain fresh pasta dough (see chart on page 8)
- 2 tablespoons coarse sea salt (to cook the pasta)

Sauce
- 3 large egg yolks
- 6 anchovy fillets
- 5 oz/150 g Mozzarella cheese, cut in $^1/_2$-inch/1-cm cubes
- 5 tablespoons butter
- salt and freshly ground white pepper to taste
- 4 tablespoons freshly grated Parmesan cheese

Prepare the tagliatelle following the instructions on pages 9–11. • Place a large pan of water over high heat with the coarse sea salt. Cover and bring to a boil. • Sauce: Beat the egg yolks in a small bowl. Add the anchovies and Mozzarella and mix well. • Cook the pasta in the pan of boiling water until al dente, about 4–5 minutes. • While the pasta is cooking, melt the butter in a large skillet (frying pan). • Drain the pasta and add to the skillet with the butter. Add 5 tablespoons of cooking water from the pasta pan and the egg mixture and toss gently until the sauce is creamy (the egg should not cook into hard pieces). • Season with pepper and sprinkle with the Parmesan. • Serve hot.

Serves 4; Preparation: 30 minutes + time to make the pasta; Cooking: 10 minutes; Level: 2

TAGLIATELLE INTEGRALI CON RUCOLA, POMODORI SECCHI, E OLIVE NERE
Whole-wheat tagliatelle with arugula, sun-dried tomatoes and black olives

Pasta
- 1 quantity whole-wheat/wholemeal pasta dough (see chart on page 8)
- 2 tablespoons coarse sea salt (to cook the pasta)

Sauce
- 12 sun-dried tomatoes
- 1 cup/250 ml hot water
- 1 bunch arugula/rocket, washed, dried, and coarsely chopped
- 4 cloves garlic, finely chopped
- 10–12 leaves fresh basil, torn
- 4 oz/125 g black olives, pitted/stoned and lightly crushed (tasty oven-dried are best)
- 4 tablespoons extra-virgin olive oil
- salt and freshly ground black pepper to taste

Prepare the whole-wheat tagliatelle following the instructions on pages 9–11. • Place a large pan of water over high heat with the coarse sea salt. Cover and bring to a boil. • Sauce: Place the tomatoes in a large bowl with the hot water. Soak for about 15 minutes, or until softened. Drain well and coarsely them chop. • Mix the arugula, tomatoes, garlic, basil, olives, oil, salt, and pepper in a bowl. • Cook the pasta in the pan of boiling water until al dente, about 4–5 minutes. • Drain the pasta and transfer to a serving bowl. Add the arugula mixture, toss gently, and serve hot.

Serves 4; Preparation: 30 minutes + time to make the pasta; Cooking: 5 minutes; Level: 2

TAGLIOLINI AL CURRY
Tagliolini with curry sauce

If you like spicy food, add more curry powder, or some crumbled dried chile pepper to the sauce.

Pasta
- 1 quantity plain fresh pasta dough (see chart on page 8)
- 2 tablespoons coarse sea salt (to cook the pasta)

Sauce
- 2 tablespoons butter
- 2 medium onions (about 10 oz/300 g), finely chopped
- salt to taste
- 1 clove garlic, finely chopped
- 4 oz/125 g ham, cut in small cubes
- 2 tablespoons hot curry powder
- $^3/_4$ cup/180 ml fresh cream
- 15 almonds, peeled and coarsely chopped

Prepare the tagliolini following the instructions on pages 9–11. • Place a large pan of water over high heat with the coarse sea salt. Cover and bring to a boil. • Sauce: Melt the butter in a large skillet (frying pan) and add the onion and a pinch of salt. Cover and cook over low heat for 20 minutes. • Add the garlic and ham and cook over medium heat until the garlic is pale gold. • Add the curry powder and stir for 2 minutes. • Stir in the almonds and cook for 2 minutes. • Pour in the cream. Bring to a boil, season with salt, and turn off the heat.• Meanwhile, cook the pasta in the pan of boiling water until al dente, about 2 minutes. • Drain the pasta and add to the skillet with the sauce. Toss gently for 1 minute, adding a little cooking water if needed. • Serve immediately.

Serves 4; Preparation: 30 minutes + time to make the pasta; Cooking: 30 minutes; Level: 2

TAGLIATELLE INTEGRALI AL LARDO
Whole-wheat tagliatelle with lard

Sauce
- 1 lb/500 g porcini (or other) wild mushrooms
- 1 tablespoon extra-virgin olive oil
- 1 clove garlic, coarsely chopped
- 1 tablespoon finely chopped rosemary
- 20 cherry tomatoes, cut in quarters
- $3^1/_2$ oz/100 g lard, cut in small cubes
- salt and freshly ground black pepper to taste

Pasta
- 1 quantity whole-wheat/wholemeal pasta dough (see chart on page 8)
- 2 tablespoons coarse sea salt (to cook the pasta)

Clean the mushrooms and place in the freezer for at least 1 hour. • Prepare the whole-wheat tagliatelle following the instructions on pages 9–11. • Place a large pan of water over high heat with the coarse sea salt. Cover and bring to a boil. • Sauce: Heat the oil in a large skillet (frying pan) over medium heat and sauté the garlic, rosemary, tomatoes, lard, salt, and pepper for 3 minutes. • Cook the pasta in the pan of boiling water until al dente, about 3–4 minutes. • Drain the pasta and add to the skillet with the sauce • Thinly slice the mushrooms straight from the freezer directly into the pan. • Serve immediately.

Serves 4; Preparation: 20 minutes + time to make the pasta;
Cooking: 10 minutes; Level: 2

TAGLIATELLE NERE CON GAMBERETTI
Black tagliatelle with shrimp

Pasta
- 1 quantity black pasta dough (see chart on page 8)
- 2 tablespoons coarse sea salt (to cook the pasta)

Sauce
- $1^1/_2$ lb/750 g shrimp, peeled, deveined, heads removed (reserve the heads), and cut in small pieces; leave 2–3 whole, to garnish
- $1^1/_4$ cups/310 ml water
- 1 small onion, cut in quarters
- small bunch of parsley, stalks whole and leaves finely chopped
- 3 tablespoons butter
- 2 cloves garlic, finely chopped
- $1^1/_4$ cups/310 ml dry white wine
- $^3/_4$ cup/180 ml fresh cream
- salt and freshly ground white pepper to taste

Prepare the tagliatelle following the instructions on pages 9–11, and 17. • Sauce: Rinse the reserved shrimp heads and place in a small saucepan with the water, onion, and parsley stalks. Bring to a boil and cook for 20 minutes. Strain, reserving the liquid. • Place a large pan of water over high heat with the coarse sea salt. Cover and bring to a boil. • Melt the butter in a large skillet (frying pan) over high heat and sauté the garlic and shrimp for 3 minutes. Remove from the skillet and set aside. • Return the skillet to high heat. Pour in the wine and cook until evaporated. Add 2–3 tablespoons of the reserved shrimp liquid. Cook for 3–4 minutes, then add the cream. Cook for 2–3 minutes, or until creamy. Season with salt and pepper. • Cook the pasta in the pan of boiling water until al dente, about 2–3 minutes. • Drain the pasta and add to the skillet with the sauce and shrimp. Toss gently. If the sauce is too dry, add 2–3 tablespoons more of the reserved shrimp liquid. • Sprinkle with the finely chopped parsley and garnish with the whole shrimp. • Serve hot.

Serves 4; Preparation: 40 minutes + time to prepare the pasta;
Cooking: 25 minutes; Level: 2

Above: Whole-wheat tagliatelle with lard

Below: Black tagliatelle with shrimp

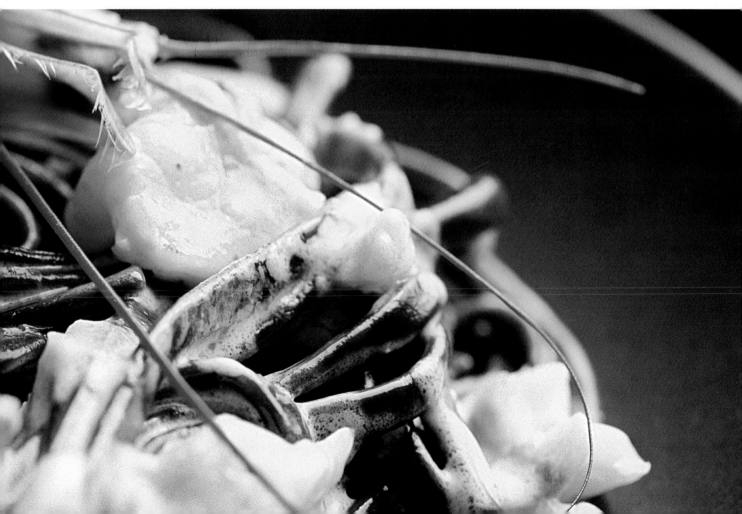

TAGLIATELLE AL RAGÙ DI AGNELLO
Tagliatelle with lamb sauce

Pasta
• 1 quantity plain fresh pasta dough (see chart on page 8)
• 2 tablespoons coarse sea salt (to cook the pasta)
Sauce
• 6 tablespoons extra-virgin olive oil
• 3 cloves garlic, finely chopped
• 1 sprig fresh rosemary
• 1 lb/500 g lamb, cut into small chunks
• scant $1/2$ cup/100 ml dry white wine
• 1 lb/500 g firm-ripe tomatoes, peeled, seeded, and coarsely chopped
• salt and freshly ground black pepper to taste

Prepare the tagliatelle following the instructions on pages 9–11. • Sauce: Heat the oil in a medium saucepan and sauté the garlic and rosemary over medium heat until the garlic is pale gold. • Add the lamb and sauté until browned all over. • Pour in the wine and cook until evaporated. • Stir in the tomatoes and season with salt and pepper. Cover and cook for about 45 minutes, or until the lamb is tender. • Place a large pan of water over high heat with the coarse sea salt. Cover and bring to a boil. • Cook the pasta in the boiling water until al dente, about 4–5 minutes. • Drain and add to the skillet with the sauce. Toss gently for 1 minute or until the sauce sticks to the pasta. • Serve hot.

Serves 4; Preparation: 45 minutes + time to make the pasta; Cooking: 1 hour; Level: 2

FARFALLE AL SALMONE FRESCO
Fresh bow pasta with salmon

Pasta
• 1 quantity plain fresh pasta dough (see chart on page 8)
• 2 tablespoons coarse sea salt (to cook the pasta)
Sauce
• 8 oz/250 g fresh salmon fillet, sliced
• 4 tablespoons extra-virgin olive oil
• 1 red onion, finely chopped
• salt to taste
• 2 tablespoons capers preserved in salt, rinsed, dried, and coarsely chopped
• 6 leaves fresh basil, torn

Prepare the farfalle pasta following the instructions on pages 9–11, 14. • Place a large pan of water over high heat with the coarse sea salt. Cover and bring to a boil. • Sauce: Cut the salmon in small cubes or strips. • Heat 2 tablespoons of oil in a large skillet (frying pan) and sauté the onion and a pinch of salt over medium-low heat for 10 minutes. • Increase the heat and add the salmon, capers, and remaining oil. Season with salt, if required – the capers will still be quite salty, so taste first. Cook for 1–2 minutes only; the salmon should not be overcooked. • Cook the pasta in the pan of boiling water until al dente, about 4–5 minutes. • Drain the pasta and add to the skillet with the salmon and basil. • Toss gently and serve hot.

Serves 4; Preparation: 40 minutes + time to make the pasta; Cooking: 20 minutes; Level: 3

Fresh bow pasta with salmon

TAJARIN ALLE ANIMELLE E NOCCIOLE
Tajarin with sweetbreads and hazelnuts

Pasta
- 2²/₃ cups/400 g unbleached flour
- 11 very fresh large egg yolks
- 2 tablespoons coarse sea salt (to cook the pasta)

Sauce
- 1 lb/500 g sweetbreads
- 1 tablespoon all-purpose/plain flour
- salt and freshly ground white pepper to taste
- 3¹/₂ oz/100 g hazelnuts, peeled and lightly toasted
- 4 tablespoons butter
- 5–6 tablespoons Marsala wine
- ²/₃ cup/150 ml fresh cream

Soak the sweetbreads in cold water for 2 hours. • Prepare the pasta dough using the flour and egg yolks and following the instructions on pages 9–11. Wrap the dough in plastic wrap (cling film) and let rest for 30 minutes. • Divide the dough into 6 pieces and roll through the machine one notch at a time down to the thinnest setting. Let dry on a lightly floured cloth for 30 minutes. • Cut into noodles about ¹/₈ inch (3 mm) wide. Shape into hanks or nests and place on a lightly floured cloth until ready to use. • Place a large pan of water over high heat with the coarse sea salt. Cover and bring to a boil. • Sauce: Place the sweetbreads in a large saucepan and cover with boiling water. Add a pinch of salt and boil for 5 minutes. Drain and place in a bowl of cold water. • When cool, drain, dry, and remove the outer membrane. Chop in small pieces and sprinkle with the flour. • Chop two-thirds of the hazelnuts finely in a food processor. Chop the remaining nuts coarsely with a knife. • Heat the butter in a large skillet (frying pan) over medium heat and sauté the sweetbreads for 3–4 minutes. • Increase the heat, add the Marsala, and cook until evaporated. • Season with salt and pepper. Add the finely chopped hazelnuts and cream and let cook for 2–3 minutes. • Cook the pasta in the pan of boiling water until al dente, about 2 minutes. • Drain the pasta and add to the skillet with the sauce. Turn off the heat and toss gently, adding 1–2 tablespoons of the cooking water if the sauce is too dry. Place in 4 individual serving dishes and garnish with the coarsely chopped hazelnuts. • Serve immediately.

Serves 4; Preparation: 45 minutes + time to make the pasta; Cooking: 30 minutes; Level: 2

TAGLIOLINI AL LIMONE CON POMODORO SECCO
Lemon tagliolini with sun-dried tomatoes

This sauce is equally good with spaghetti. Make a double quantity and conserve half in a jar in the refrigerator. Covered with a thin veil of extra-virgin olive oil, the sauce will keep for about one week. For spaghetti, double the quantity of lemon juice and zest and don't add them to the sauce until just before use.

Pasta
- 2 cups/300 g unbleached flour
- 3 very fresh large eggs
- 2 tablespoons fresh lemon juice
- 2 tablespoons finely grated lemon zest
- 2 tablespoons coarse sea salt (to cook the pasta)

Sauce
- 2¹/₂ oz/75 g sun-dried tomatoes
- 2 tablespoons white wine vinegar
- 2–3 tablespoons water
- juice and zest of ¹/₂ lemon (zest should be cut into a long, thin length)
- 4 tablespoons extra-virgin olive oil
- salt and freshly ground white pepper to taste

Prepare the tagliolini following the instructions on pages 9–11, adding the lemon juice and zest to the eggs. Wrap the dough in plastic wrap (cling film) and let rest for 30 minutes. Divide the dough into 6 pieces. Roll it through the machine one notch at a time down to the thinnest setting. Cut the tagliolini with a knife into noodles about ¹/₄ inch (6 mm) wide. Shape in nests and leave to dry for 30 minutes on a lightly floured cloth. • Place a large pan of water over high heat with the coarse sea salt. Cover and bring to a boil. • Sauce: Place the sun-dried tomatoes in a small bowl with the vinegar and water. Soak for 15 minutes, stirring occasionally. • Drain, squeezing out the moisture. Finely chop with a knife or in a food processor, leaving a few whole or coarsely chopped to garnish. • Place in a serving dish and add the juice and zest of the lemon and the oil. Season with salt and pepper—not too much salt, because the tomatoes will already be fairly salty. Taste first. • Cook the pasta in the pan of boiling water until al dente, about 2–3 minutes. • Drain the pasta and add to the serving dish with the sauce. • Toss gently and garnish with the whole or coarsely chopped tomatoes. • Serve immediately.

Serves 4; Preparation: 50 minutes + time to make the pasta; Cooking: 2–3 minutes; Level: 2

Lemon tagliolini with sun-dried tomatoes

FAZZOLETTI AL BELUGA

Fresh pasta with caviar

Pasta
- 1 quantity plain fresh pasta dough (see chart on page 8)
- 2 tablespoons coarse sea salt (to cook the pasta)

Sauce
- $^1/_2$ cup/125 ml extra-virgin olive oil
- 4 tablespoons coarse dry bread crumbs
- 3 oz/90 g Beluga caviar
- 3 shallots, finely chopped
- 2 tablespoons chives, finely chopped
- 2 tablespoons capers preserved in salt, rinsed, dried, and finely chopped
- 1 tablespoon finely chopped parsley
- 2 hard-boiled eggs, mashed with a fork
- salt to taste

Prepare the pasta dough following the instructions on pages 9–11. • Divide the pasta into 5 pieces and roll them through the machine one notch at a time down to the thinnest setting. Dry the sheets of pasta on a lightly floured cloth for 30 minutes. • Cut into strips about $^3/_4$ inch (2 cm) wide and then into triangles with 2-inch (5-cm) bases. • Place a large pan of water over high heat with the coarse sea salt. Cover and bring to a boil. • Sauce: Heat half the oil in a small skillet (frying pan) and sauté the bread crumbs until browned. • Place the caviar, shallots, chives, capers, parsley, remaining oil, and eggs in a large serving dish and stir gently. Place the serving dish over the pasta pan to heat. • Cook the pasta in the pan of boiling water until al dente, about 4 minutes. • Drain the pasta and add to the bowl with the sauce. Toss gently and decorate with the toasted bread crumbs. • Serve immediately.

Serves 4; Preparation: 30 minutes + time to make the pasta; Cooking: 4 minutes; Level: 2the pasta; Cooking: 20 minutes; Level: 2

MALTAGLIATI FREDDI AL TONNO, CAPPERI E LIMONE

Chilled maltagliati with tuna, capers, and lemon

Pasta
- 1 quantity plain fresh pasta dough (see chart on page 8)
- 4 tablespoons coarse sea salt

Sauce
- 14 oz/400 g tuna preserved in olive oil, drained
- $2^1/_2$ oz/75 g capers preserved in salt, rinsed, dried, and finely chopped
- 2 tablespoons finely chopped parsley
- 1 tablespoon finely chopped fresh mint
- $^1/_2$ clove garlic, finely chopped
- juice of 1 lemon
- 6 tablespoons extra-virgin olive oil
- salt and freshly ground black pepper to taste

Prepare the maltagliati pasta following the instructions on pages 9–11, 14. • Place a large pan of water over high heat with half the coarse sea salt. Cover and bring to a boil. • Sauce: Place the tuna in a medium bowl and mash with the back of a fork. Add the capers, parsley, mint, garlic, lemon juice, and 4 tablespoons of oil and mix well. Set aside. • Cook the pasta in the pan of boiling water until al dente, about 4–5 minutes. • Drain well and place in a large bowl of cold water with the remaining coarse sea salt and the remaining oil. Leave until cold. • Drain well and place in a large bowl. Add the tuna sauce, season with salt and pepper, and toss gently. • Refrigerate for at least 15 minutes before serving. Do not store in the refrigerator for more than 12 hours, as the delicate flavors of the pasta will spoil.

Serves 4; Preparation: 25 minutes + time to make the pasta + time to cool and chill; Cooking: 4–5 minutes; Level: 2

TAGLIOLINI SCAMPI E RADICCHIO

Tagliolini with prawns and radicchio

Pasta
- 1 quantity plain fresh pasta dough (see chart on page 8)
- 2 tablespoons coarse sea salt (to cook the pasta)

Sauce
- 1 lb/500 g Dublin Bay prawns
- 3 tablespoons butter
- 1 clove garlic, finely chopped
- 4 tablespoons brandy
- 1 medium tomato, peeled, seeded, and chopped
- salt and freshly ground white pepper to taste
- $^3/_4$ cup/180 ml fresh cream
- 8 oz/250 g Treviso radicchio, cut in julienne strips (matchsticks)

Prepare the tagliolini following the instructions on pages 9–11. • Place a large pan of water over high heat with the coarse sea salt. Cover and bring to a boil. • Sauce: Peel the prawns and chop the bodies coarsely. Remove the flesh from the heads and claws as well. • Melt the butter in a large skillet (frying pan) and sauté the garlic with the prawn meat from the heads and claws. • Pour in the brandy and cook until evaporated. • Add the tomato and cook for 3 minutes. Add the remaining prawn meat. Season with salt and pepper and cook over low heat for 1–2 minutes. Add the cream and cook until reduced. • Cook the pasta in the pan of boiling water until al dente, about 2 minutes. Drain the pasta and add to the skillet with the prawns. • Add the radicchio, toss gently, and serve immediately.

Serves 4; Preparation: 45 minutes + time to make the pasta; Cooking: 15 minutes; Level: 2

PAPPARDELLE AL CINGHIALE

Pappardelle with wild boar sauce

Pasta
- 1 quantity durum wheat pasta dough (see chart on page 8)
- 2 tablespoons coarse sea salt (to cook the pasta)

Sauce
- 4 tablespoons extra-virgin olive oil
- 1 small onion, finely chopped
- 1 carrot, finely chopped
- 1 stalk celery, finely chopped
- salt and freshly ground black pepper to taste
- 1 lb/500 g wild boar meat, coarsely chopped
- $^2/_3$ cup/180 ml dry red wine
- 1 cup/250 ml meat stock (see page 97)
- 2 cloves garlic, finely chopped
- 1 sprig fresh sage, finely chopped
- 1 sprig fresh rosemary, finely chopped

Prepare the pappardelle following the instructions on pages 9–11. • Sauce: Heat the oil in a cast-iron or other heavy-bottomed casserole and add the onion, carrot, celery, and a pinch of salt. Cover and cook for 10 minutes, stirring often. • Add the wild boar and sauté over high heat until lightly browned. Season with salt and pepper. Pour in the wine and cook until evaporated. • Pour in $^3/_4$ cup (180 ml) of stock and cover and cook over low heat for 2 hours. Stir often, adding more stock if the sauce dries out too much. • Place a large pan of water over high heat with the coarse sea salt. Cover and bring to a boil. Cook the pasta in the pan of boiling water until al dente, about 6–7 minutes. • While the pasta is cooking, remove the wild boar meat from the pan and chop finely with a large knife. Return to the pan and add the garlic, sage, and rosemary. Season with salt and pepper. • Drain the pasta and place in a serving dish. Pour the sauce over the top and toss gently. • Serve hot.

Serves 4; Preparation: 30 minutes + time to prepare the pasta; Cooking: 2 hours 30 minutes; Level: 2

TAGLIOLINI ALLA CARBONARA DI PESCE
Spinach tagliolini with seafood and eggs

Pasta
- 1 quantity colored (spinach) pasta dough (see chart on page 8)
- 2 tablespoons coarse sea salt (to cook the pasta) + extra to soak the clams

Sauce
- 3 lb/1.5 kg mixed mussels and clams, in shell
- $1/2$ cup/125 ml dry white wine
- 4 tablespoons extra-virgin olive oil
- 3 cloves garlic, finely chopped
- 7 oz/200 g shrimp tails
- 2 tablespoons finely chopped parsley
- 3 egg yolks
- freshly ground black pepper to taste

Prepare the tagliolini following the instructions on pages 9–11, and 17. • Soak the mussels and clams in a large bowl of water with coarse sea salt (15 g for each liter of water) for 1 hour. Discard any that are open or broken. • Place a large pan of water over high heat with the coarse sea salt. Cover and bring to a boil. • Sauce: Rinse the shellfish thoroughly and scrub the beards off the mussels with a wire brush. Discard any that are open or broken. • To open the shellfish, place a handful or two in a large skillet (frying pan) with 2 tablespoons of wine over high heat. Cook until they have opened. Repeat until all the shellfish are open. Discard any that do not open. • Remove the mollusks from their shells (leave a few in the shell to garnish). • Strain the liquid remaining in the skillet and reserve. • Heat the oil in the skillet over medium-high heat and sauté the garlic, shrimp tails, and parsley for 3 minutes. Turn off the heat. • Beat the egg yolks in a serving dish and season with pepper. Add 2 tablespoons of the reserved cooking liquid. • Cook the pasta in the pan of boiling water until very al dente, about 3–4 minutes. • Drain the pasta and add to the skillet with the seafood. Toss gently for 2–3 minutes over medium heat then transfer to the serving dish with the eggs. Toss gently until the sauce is creamy. Season with a little more pepper, if liked. • Serve immediately.

Serves 4; Preparation: 45 minutes + 1 hour to soak the seafood + time to prepare the pasta; Cooking: 20 minutes; Level: 3

TAGLIATELLE DI CECI AL BACCALÀ
Garbanzo bean tagliatelle with stockfish

Pasta
- 7 oz/200 g garbanzo bean/chickpea flour
- $1^1/3$ cups/200 g unbleached flour
- 4 large eggs
- 2 tablespoons coarse sea salt (to cook the pasta)

Sauce
- 1 lb/500 g soaked stockfish
- 5 tablespoons extra-virgin olive oil
- 2 cloves garlic, finely chopped
- 1 sprig rosemary, finely chopped
- 5 oz/150 g Swiss chard, stalks removed and cut in strips
- $1/2$ cup/125 g canned, chopped tomatoes
- salt and freshly ground white pepper to taste

Prepare the pasta dough with both flours and the eggs following the instructions on pages 9–11. Wrap the dough in plastic wrap (cling film) and let rest for 30 minutes. • Divide the dough into 6 pieces and roll through the machine one notch at a time down to the thinnest setting. Cut the tagliatelle with a knife into noodles about $1/4$-inch (6 mm) wide. Dry on a lightly floured work surface for 30 minutes. • Sauce: Place a large pan of water over high heat and bring to a boil. Remove from the heat and add the stockfish. Let soak for 15 minutes. • Drain the stockfish, remove the skin and bones, and crumble the flesh with your hands. • Place a large pan of water over high heat with the coarse sea salt. Cover and bring to a boil. • Heat the oil in a large skillet (frying pan) and sauté the garlic and rosemary for 3 minutes. • Add the Swiss chard and tomatoes and cook for 5 minutes. Cover and cook over low heat for 10 more minutes, adding a little water if the sauce dries out too much. Season with salt and pepper. • Add the stockfish and cook for 5 more minutes. • Meanwhile, cook the pasta in the pan of boiling water until very al dente, about 2–3 minutes. • Drain and add to the skillet with the sauce. Toss gently, adding a little of the cooking water if the sauce is too dry. • Serve hot.

Serves 4; Preparation: 45 minutes + time to prepare the pasta; Cooking: 40 minutes; Level: 2

Above: Spinach tagliatelle with seafood and eggs

Below: Garbanzo bean tagliatelle with stockfish

FETTUCCINE ALLA BORRAGINE

Fettuccine with borage

Pasta

- 10 oz/300 g borage leaves
- salt to taste
- 2 cups/300 g unbleached flour
- 3 very fresh large eggs
- 2 tablespoons coarse sea salt (to cook the pasta)

Sauce

- 5–6 tablespoons butter
- $^3/_4$ cup/90 g freshly grated Parmesan cheese

Pasta: Rinse the borage leaves thoroughly under cold running water. Bring 1 quart (1 liter) of water to a boil in a saucepan with a generous pinch of salt and cook the borage for about 20 minutes. Drain and let cool. • Chop the borage in a food processor until very fine, then strain it. Place in a clean cloth and squeeze well to eliminate excess moisture. • Beat the eggs in a bowl and mix in the borage. • Prepare the pasta dough following the instructions on pages 9–11, and 17, using the flour and borage-flavored eggs to obtain a fairly firm dough. Knead for 20 minutes, then wrap in plastic wrap (cling film) and let rest for 30 minutes. • Divide the dough in 4 pieces and roll each one through the machine one notch at a time down to the thinnest setting. • Cut the pasta into noodles about $^1/_4$ x 25 cm (6 mm x 25 cm). Dry the pasta on a lightly floured cloth for 30 minutes. • Place a large pan of water over high heat with the coarse sea salt. Cover and bring to a boil. • Cook the pasta in the pan of boiling water until al dente, about 1–2 minutes. • While the pasta is cooking, melt the butter over medium heat until brown. • Drain the pasta and transfer to a heated serving dish. Drizzle in the butter, sprinkle with the Parmesan, and toss gently. • Serve hot.

Serves 4; Preparation: 15 minutes + time to make the pasta; Cooking: 25 minutes; Level: 2

STRACCI AI FIORI DI ZUCCA

Stracci with zucchini flowers

Pasta

- 1 quantity plain fresh pasta dough (see chart on page 8)
- 2 tablespoons coarse sea salt (to cook the pasta)

Sauce

- 1 tablespoon extra-virgin olive oil
- $1^1/_2$ oz/45 g prosciutto/Parma ham, cut in julienne strips (matchsticks)
- $^3/_4$ cup/180 ml fresh cream
- $^1/_8$ teaspoon ground saffron
- salt to taste
- 12 zucchini/courgette flowers, sliced in 4 lengthwise

To serve

- 4 zucchini flowers
- 1 tablespoon finely chopped parsley

Prepare the stracci pasta following the instructions on pages 9–11, 14. • Place a large pan of water over high heat with the coarse sea salt. Cover and bring to a boil. • Sauce: Heat the oil in a large skillet (frying pan) and sauté the prosciutto. Cook for 2 minutes. • Pour in the cream and cook for 3 minutes. • Add the saffron and stir well. Season with salt and turn off the heat. • Cook the pasta in the pan of boiling water until al dente, about 4–5 minutes. • Reheat the sauce and add the sliced zucchini flowers. • Drain the pasta and add to the skillet with the sauce. Toss gently for 1 minute. • Serve immediately in individual serving dishes, each one decorated with a zucchini flower and a sprinkling of parsley.

Serves 4; Preparation: 30 minutes + time to make the pasta; Cooking:15 minutes; Level: 2

Stracci with zucchini flowers

TAGLIATELLE ROSSE ALLE OLIVE
Beet tagliatelle with olives

Pasta
- 1 quantity colored (beet) pasta dough (see chart on page 8)
- 2 tablespoons coarse sea salt (to cook the pasta)

Sauce
- 3 tablespoons extra-virgin olive oil
- 2 tablespoons butter
- 14 oz/400 g sweet black olives, pitted and coarsely chopped
- 1 small fresh chile pepper (not too spicy), seeded, cut half in rounds and half in julienne strips (matchsticks)
- salt to taste
- 1 cup/125 g freshly grated Parmesan cheese

Prepare the beet tagliatelle following the instructions on pages 9–11, and 17. • Place a large pan of water over high heat with the coarse sea salt. Cover and bring to a boil. • Sauce: Heat the oil and butter in a large skillet (frying pan) and add the olives and chile pepper. Season with salt. Sauté for 4–5 minutes. • Cook the pasta in the pan of boiling water until al dente, about 4–5 minutes. • Drain the pasta and add to the skillet with the olive sauce. Toss gently, adding 1–2 tablespoons of cooking water, if needed. • Remove from heat and sprinkle with the Parmesan. • Serve immediately.

Serves 4; Preparation: 25 minutes + time to make the pasta; Cooking: 10 minutes; Level: 2

TAGLIERINI FREDDI
Cool taglierini

Sauce
- 10 oz/300 g fresh salmon, cut in $1/4$-inch/$1/2$-cm thick slices
- juice of 1 lemon
- salt and freshly ground white pepper to taste
- 4 medium ripe tomatoes, peeled, seeded, and chopped
- 1 scallion/spring onion, finely chopped (both the green and white parts)
- 4 celery leaves, in chiffonade
- 6 tablespoons extra-virgin olive oil
- 2 tablespoons balsamic vinegar

Pasta
- 1 quantity mixed durum wheat pasta dough (see chart on page 8)
- 2 tablespoons coarse sea salt (to cook the pasta)

Sauce: Cut the salmon in julienne strips (matchsticks). Place in a glass bowl and season with the lemon juice, salt, and pepper. Cover with plastic wrap (cling film) and marinate in the refrigerator for 2 hours, stirring occasionally. • Prepare the taglierini following the instructions on pages 9–11. • Place the tomatoes in a colander and sprinkle with 1 teaspoon of salt. Leave to drain for 30 minutes. • Place a large pan of water over high heat with the coarse sea salt. Cover and bring to a boil. Cook the pasta in the pan of boiling water until al dente, about 2–3 minutes. • Combine the marinated salmon and drained tomatoes in a serving dish with the scallion, celery leaves, oil, and balsamic vinegar. • Drain the pasta and pass the colander under cold running water. Drain well and add to the serving dish with the sauce. Toss gently. • Keep in the refrigerator until ready to serve.

Serves 4; Preparation: 30 minutes + time to prepare the pasta + 2 hours to marinate the salmon; Cooking: 2–3 minutes; Level: 2

Above: Beetroot tagliatelle with olives

Below: Cool taglierini

LASAGNA AL PIATTO ALLE VERDURE MISTE
Unbaked lasagne with spring vegetables

Pasta
- $1/2$ quantity plain fresh pasta dough (see chart on page 8)
- 2 tablespoons coarse sea salt (to cook the pasta)
- 1 tablespoon extra-virgin olive oil (to cook the pasta)

Sauce
- 3 quarts/3 liters cold water
- 1 small onion, sliced
- 1 stalk celery, chopped
- 1 carrot, sliced
- 1 tomato, cut in half
- 3 sprigs parsley
- 3 leaves fresh basil
- 1 clove garlic
- 1 bay leaf
- 10 filled pea pods
- a few artichoke leaves
- a few stalks of asparagus
- 1 tablespoon coarse sea salt
- 4 tablespoons butter
- scant $1/2$ cup/75 g all-purpose/plain flour
- salt and freshly ground white pepper to taste
- pinch of freshly ground nutmeg

Filling
- about $1/2$ cup/125 ml extra-virgin olive oil
- 1 shallot, thinly sliced
- $2^1/2$ oz/75 g lard, cut in small cubes
- 8 oz/250 g fresh fava/broad beans
- 7 oz/200 g peas
- 4 lettuce leaves, thinly sliced
- 2 tablespoons finely chopped parsley
- 1 tablespoon sugar
- salt and freshly ground white pepper to taste
- 4 artichokes
- 1 lemon
- 3 cloves garlic, finely chopped
- $1^1/4$ lb/625 g asparagus, cleaned
- 1 tablespoon finely chopped mint
- $3/4$ cup/90 g freshly grated Pecorino cheese

Prepare the lasagne following the instructions on pages 9–11. Cut the sheets of lasagne into pieces measuring about 6 inches (15 cm) square. You will need 16 pieces. • Sauce: Place the water in a large saucepan with the onion, celery, carrot, tomato, parsley, basil, garlic, bay leaf, pea pods, artichoke leaves, and asparagus. Add the coarse sea salt and bring to a boil. Simmer for 40 minutes. • Remove from the heat and strain, reserving the stock. • Melt the butter in a medium saucepan and add the flour. Stir over medium heat for 2 minutes, then pour in 1 quart (1 liter) of the strained vegetable stock and beat energetically with a wire whisk. Bring to a boil, stirring constantly. Season with nutmeg, salt, and

pepper. • Simmer, stirring often, for 15 minutes. Turn off heat. • Filling: Heat 3 tablespoons of oil in a medium saucepan. Add the shallot, lard, fava beans, peas, lettuce, 1 tablespoon of parsley, the sugar, and 2 cups (500 ml) of the vegetable stock. Partially cover and bring to a boil. Cook over medium-low heat for 40 minutes, or until the vegetables are tender. Add more stock if the filling dries out. Season with salt and pepper. • Remove the tough outer leaves from the artichokes and chop off the top third of the leaves. Trim and peel the stalk. Cut the artichokes in half and remove any fuzzy choke. Soak in cold water with the lemon for 5 minutes to stop them from turning black. • Slice the artichokes thinly lengthwise and return to the bowl of cold water and lemon. • Heat 4 tablespoons of oil in a large skillet (frying pan) and add 2 cloves of garlic, the remaining parsley, mint, artichokes, and 1 cup (250 ml) of vegetable stock. Season with salt and pepper. Cover and cook for about 25 minutes, or until the artichokes are tender. • Trim the tough parts off the bottoms of the asparagus stalks (these can be used in the stock). Separate the stalks from the tender tips. Cut the stalks into pieces about $1/2$ inch (1 cm) long. • Heat 3 tablespoons of oil with 1 clove of finely chopped garlic in a large skillet. Add the asparagus stalks and sauté for 3–4 minutes. Cover with stock and cook for 4 minutes. Add the tips, cover and cook for about 15 minutes, or until tender. Add more stock to keep moist if necessary. • Place a large pan of water over high heat with the coarse sea salt and oil. Cover and bring to a boil. • Cook the sheets of lasagne following the instructions on page 66. • Heat individual serving plates. Make sure that the sauce and three fillings are also hot. • Place 2 tablespoons of sauce in the bottom of each serving plate. Cook 4 pieces of pasta, drain well and place one in each plate. Cover with the asparagus and a thin layer of sauce. Top with a piece of pasta and cover with the peas and a thin layer of sauce and Pecorino. Cover with pasta, the artichokes, a thin layer of sauce, and Pecorino. Top with the last layer of pasta, sauce, and Pecorino. • Serve immediately.

Serves 6–8: Preparation: 2 hours + time to make the pasta; Cooking: 1 hour 30 minutes; Level 3

Unbaked lasagne with spring vegetables

STRACCI DI SARACENO CON PATATE E LATTUGA
Fresh buckwheat pasta with potatoes and lettuce

Pasta
- 1 quantity buckwheat pasta dough (see chart on page 8)
- 2 tablespoons coarse sea salt (to cook the pasta)

Sauce
- 1 lb/500 g potatoes, peeled and cut in small cubes
- 3^1/$_2$ oz/100 g butter
- 1 onion, finely chopped
- 4–6 leaves fresh sage
- salt and freshly ground white pepper to taste
- 14 oz/400 g lettuce, well washed and cut in strips
- 4 tablespoons freshly grated Parmesan cheese
- 2 oz/60 g Gruyere or Swiss cheese, thinly sliced

Prepare the stracci pasta following the instructions on pages 9–11, and 13. • Place a large pan of water over high heat with the coarse sea salt. Cover and bring to a boil. • Add the potatoes and cook until very well cooked, about 30 minutes. • Add the pasta to the pan with the potatoes after they have been cooking for about 25 minutes. The pasta will be cooked in 4–5 minutes. Sauce: Heat the butter in a large skillet (frying pan) and add the onion and sage. Season with salt and pepper. Cover and cook over low heat for 15 minutes. • Add the lettuce and stir until it has wilted, about 5 minutes. Add a little water from the pasta pot if the mixture dries out too much. • Heat a large deep serving bowl. • Use a slotted spoon to remove the potatoes and pasta. Drain well and place a layer in the bottom of the serving dish. Cover with a layer of cheeses and lettuce sauce. Repeat until all the ingredients are in the dish. • Season well with white pepper and serve hot.

Serves 4; Preparation: 1 hour 15 minutes + 30 minutes to rest; Cooking: 45 minutes; Level: 2

TAGLIATELLE AL CACAO CON PEPERONI
Chocolate tagliatelle with bell peppers

Pasta
- 1 quantity aromatic (cocoa) pasta dough (see chart on page 8)
- 2 tablespoons coarse sea salt (to cook the pasta)

Sauce
- 4 tablespoons extra-virgin olive oil
- 1 lb/500 g yellow bell peppers/capsicums, cut in strips
- salt to taste
- 8 oz/250 g red bell peppers/capsicums, cut in ^{1}/$_2$-cm squares
- 4 tablespoons fresh cream

Prepare the chocolate tagliatelle pasta following the instructions on pages 9–11. • Place a large pan of water over high heat with the coarse sea salt. Cover and bring to a boil. • Sauce: Heat half the oil in a large skillet (frying pan) and add the yellow bell pepper. Season with salt and cover and cook over medium heat until the bell pepper is tender. • Transfer to a food processor and chop it finely. • Season with salt and return to the skillet. • Heat the remaining oil in a separate skillet and sauté the red bell pepper over high heat until tender-crunchy, about 3–4 minutes. • Cook the pasta in the pan of boiling water until al dente, about 4 minutes. • Drain the pasta and add to the skillet with the yellow purée. Add the cream and toss gently for 1 minute. • Serve immediately in individual serving dishes, each one decorated with a quarter of the red bell pepper.

Serves 4; Preparation: 20 minutes + time to make the pasta; Cooking: 20 minutes; Level: 2

Above: Fresh buckwheat pasta with potatoes and lettuce

Below: Chocolate tagliatelle with bell peppers

Baked

Baked pasta dishes are made with delicately flavored sheets of freshly rolled pasta, then layered with scrumptious fillings and sauces, and topped with cheese before being baked to perfection in a hot oven. Lasagne and cannelloni are probably the best known types of baked pasta dishes, but there are many other equally enticing recipes. This chapter includes 27 of our all-time favorites, ranging from classic *Baked cannelloni* and *Lasagne with pesto* to more inventive dishes, such as *Rosettes with squid sauce* and *Tagliatelle cake*.

Above: Cannelloni with mushrooms (page 70)
Left: Baked pasta roses (page 68)

Blanching lasagne sheets

Sheets of pasta for lasagne and many other baked pasta dishes need to be blanched for a few seconds in boiling water, then cooled in cold water and squeezed. This partial cooking process is necessary for the success of your finished dish.

Salt and oil

When blanching lasagne sheets, add 1 teaspoon each of coarse sea salt and extra-virgin olive oil for every liter of water. We suggest you use 3–4 liters of water to blanch the sheets and about the same measure (with the same amount of salt and oil) to cool them.

❶

Bring a large pan of water to a boil. Add the salt and olive oil. Add the lasagne sheets carefully one at a time.

❷

After 3–5 seconds, depending on the thickness of the pasta, scoop the sheet of pasta out using a large slotted spoon. Transfer to a large bowl of cold water with salt and oil. If the water warms up, add a few cubes of ice.

❸

Use a slotted spoon to remove the sheet of pasta from the cold water after a few seconds.

❹

Remove the excess water from each sheet by squeezing them very carefully.

❺

Lay the blanched pasta sheets out on a clean damp cloth. Make sure they do not overlap, as they will stick together.

Pasta with stripes and motifs

With just a little extra time and effort you can create some very attractive designs for sheets of pasta. These can be used to add a special touch to lasagne (be sure to place the decorated sheet of pasta on top) and for many filled pasta shapes too.

Striped pasta

To make the dough for striped pasta you will need to prepare the four different types of pasta first (see the chart on page 8). Make 1 quantity of plain pasta and $1/3$ quantities of the other three.

❶

Place an attractively shaped, slightly damp leaf of parsley at one end of a lasagne sheet. Fold the other end over the top.

❷

Roll the sheet through the pasta machine at the second thinnest setting and then again at the thinnest setting.

❸

You will end up with an attractive green parsley leaf motif at the center of the sheet of lasagne.

❶

Roll the pasta dough into sheets about 4 x 6 inches (10 x 15 cm). Cut the colored sheets into strips about $3/4$ inch (2 cm) wide and lay on the plain pasta.

❷

Roll the sheet very carefully through the pasta machine at the third thinnest setting. Do not roll any thinner than this.

❸

Use the striped pasta to make an eyecatching lasagne or special filled shapes.

ROSE DI PASTA
Baked pasta roses

Pasta
- $3/4$ quantity plain fresh pasta dough (see chart on page 8)
- 2 tablespoons coarse sea salt (to cook the pasta)
- 2 tablespoons extra-virgin olive oil (to cook the pasta)

Filling
- 10 oz/300 g thinly sliced ham
- 10 oz/300 g thinly sliced Edam cheese

Béchamel sauce
- 3 tablespoons butter
- $1/3$ cup/50 g all-purpose/plain flour
- pinch of freshly grated nutmeg
- $2^2/3$ cups/650 ml milk
- salt and freshly ground white pepper to taste
- 2 tablespoons butter, cut up
- bay leaves and parsley, to garnish

Prepare the pasta dough following the instructions on pages 9–11. Set aside to rest for 30 minutes. • Divide the dough into 5 pieces. Roll it through the machine one notch at a time down to the thinnest setting. Let dry on a lightly floured cloth for 30 minutes. • Place a large pan of water over high heat with half the coarse sea salt and oil. Cover and bring to a boil. • Béchamel sauce: Melt the butter in a medium saucepan, then stir in the flour and nutmeg. Cook for 3–4 minutes, stirring constantly, then add the milk all at once. Season with salt and pepper. Bring to a boil, stirring constantly. • Simmer for 10 minutes, stirring almost continuously, then remove from the heat. • Cut the pasta into 4 x 6-inch (10 x 15-cm) rectangles. • Blanch the rectangles of pasta as you would for lasagne, following the instructions on page 66. Drain each piece and place in a bowl of cold water with the remaining coarse sea salt and oil. Drain again and place on a damp cloth with edges overlapping to form a large rectangle. • Preheat the oven to 450°F/225°C/gas 7. • Butter a large ovenproof baking dish. • Spread the Béchamel over the pasta and cover with the slices of ham and cheese. • Use the cloth to help you roll the pasta up into a loose roll. Cut into slices just over 1 inch (3 cm) thick. • Bake for 20 minutes, or until the "roses" are nicely browned. • Garnish with bay leaves and parsley and serve hot.

Serves 6; Preparation: 45 minutes + time to make the pasta; Cooking: 45 minutes; Level 3

TIMBALLO DI LASAGNE VERDI
Baked spinach lasagne

Game sauce
- scant $1/2$ cup/100 g butter
- 4 tablespoons extra-virgin olive oil
- 2 carrots, cut in small cubes
- 1 stalk celery, cut in small cubes
- 1 white onion, cut in small cubes
- 5 small game birds (thrush, ortolan, lark), cleaned and ready to cook (season inside with salt and pepper)
- 3 oz/90 g dried porcini mushrooms, soaked in cold water for 2 hours, drained (reserving the water), and chopped
- 1 cup/125 g freshly grated Parmesan cheese
- $3^1/2$ oz/100 g prosciutto/Parma ham, cut in julienne strips (matchsticks)
- salt to taste

Pasta
- $1^1/4$ quantities colored (spinach) pasta dough (see chart on page 8)
- 2 tablespoons coarse sea salt (to cook the pasta)
- 2 tablespoons extra-virgin olive oil (to cook the pasta)

Béchamel sauce
- 3 tablespoons butter
- $1/3$ cup/50 g all-purpose/plain flour
- pinch of freshly grated nutmeg
- 2 cups/500 ml milk
- salt and freshly ground white pepper to taste

Game sauce: Melt 3 tablespoons of butter with the oil in a large saucepan and add the carrots, celery, onion, and game birds. Cover with a piece of waxed paper, then cover with the lid. Cook over very low heat for 3 hours. Check the pan from time to time, adding a little water if it dries out too much. • Prepare the pasta dough following the instructions on pages 9–11. Set aside to rest for 30 minutes. • Divide the dough into 6 pieces. Roll it through the machine one notch at a time down to the thinnest setting. Let dry on a lightly floured cloth for 30 minutes. • Place a large pan of water over high heat with half the coarse sea salt and oil. Cover and bring to a boil. • Béchamel sauce: Melt the butter in a medium saucepan, then stir in the flour and nutmeg. Cook for 3–4 minutes, stirring constantly, then add the milk all at once. Season with salt and pepper. Bring to a boil, stirring constantly. • Simmer for 10 minutes, stirring almost continuously, then remove from the heat. • Cut the pasta into 6 x 8-inch (15 x 20-cm) rectangles. • Blanch the rectangles of pasta as you would for lasagne, following the instructions on page 66. Drain each piece and place in a bowl of cold water with the remaining coarse sea salt and oil. Drain again and place on a damp cloth. • Remove the birds from the saucepan. Bone them and cut the flesh into small pieces. • When the cooking juices have cooled, skim off the fat on the surface. • Melt a heaping tablespoon of butter in a small saucepan. Add the mushrooms and little of the water they were soaked in. Cover and cook over low heat for 30 minutes. • Preheat the oven to 350°F/180°C/gas 4. • Butter 6 small ovenproof baking dishes. • Cover each dish with a piece of pasta that has been dipped into the cooking juices. Leave the edges overlapping the sides of the dishes. Fill each one with 2 tablespoons of bird meat, 2 tablespoons of the birds' cooking juices, some Béchamel, and a sprinkling of Parmesan. Cover with another sheet of pasta dipped in the mushrooms' cooking juices. Cover with a layer of mushrooms, some Béchamel, and a sprinkling of Parmesan. • Cover with another sheet of pasta and spread with prosciutto, Béchamel, and a sprinkling of Parmesan. • Close the overlapping edges over the dish and drizzle with a little of the birds' cooking juices. Dot with the remaining butter. • Bake for 20–30 minutes, or until nicely browned on top. • Let rest 10 minutes before serving.

Serves 6; Preparation: 50 minutes + time to make the pasta; Cooking: 4 hours; Level 3

CANNELLONI RIPIENI DI CARNE
Baked cannelloni

Pasta
• 1 quantity plain fresh pasta dough (see chart on page 8)
• 2 tablespoons coarse sea salt (to cook the pasta)
• 2 tablespoons extra-virgin olive oil (to cook the pasta)
Meat sauce
• 4 tablespoons extra-virgin olive oil
• 1 small onion, finely chopped
• 1 stalk celery, finely chopped
• 1 small carrot, finely chopped
• 1 tablespoon finely chopped parsley
• 3 oz/90 g Italian sausages, crumbled
• 4 oz/125 g ground/minced beef
• 5 oz/150 g chicken livers, cleaned and finely chopped
• 1 tablespoon all-purpose/plain flour
• $1/2$ cup/125 ml Marsala wine
• 1 cup/250 g canned, chopped tomatoes
• $1/2$ cup/125 ml beef stock
• salt and freshly ground black pepper to taste
Béchamel sauce
• 3 tablespoons butter
• $1/3$ cup/50 g all-purpose/plain flour
• pinch of freshly grated nutmeg
• $2 2/3$ cups/650 ml milk
• salt and freshly ground white pepper to taste
Filling
• 6 tablespoons butter
• $1/2$ onion, finely chopped
• 10 oz/300 g lean ground/minced veal or beef
• $3/4$ cup/90 g finely chopped ham
• 3 oz/90 g ground/minced chicken breast
• 6 tablespoons dry white wine
• 6 tablespoons Meat stock (see page 97)

• salt and freshly ground white pepper to taste
• 3 tablespoons Béchamel sauce (see above)
• 1 egg
• 4 tablespoons freshly grated Parmesan cheese
• $1/8$ teaspoon freshly grated nutmeg
• 4 tablespoons butter, cut up

Prepare the pasta dough following the instructions on pages 9–11. Set aside to rest for 30 minutes. • Meat sauce: Heat the oil in a medium saucepan over high heat. Add the onion, celery, carrot, and parsley and sauté for 4 minutes. • Add the sausages and cook over medium-low heat until the fat in the sausages has melted. • Increase the heat and sauté the beef until browned all over. • Add the chicken livers and cook for 3 minutes. • Sprinkle with the flour and cook for 3 minutes. • Pour in the Marsala and cook until evaporated. • Stir in the tomatoes and stock and season with salt and pepper. Cover and cook over low heat for about 1 hour, stirring often. • Divide the pasta dough into 6 pieces. Roll it through the machine one notch at a time down to the second thinnest setting. Let dry on a lightly floured cloth for 30 minutes. • Cut the dough into 4 x 7-inch (10 x 18-cm) rectangles. • Blanch the rectangles of pasta as you would for lasagne, following the instructions on page 66. Drain each piece and place in a bowl of cold water with the remaining coarse sea salt and oil. Drain again and place on a damp cloth. • Béchamel sauce: Melt the butter in a medium saucepan, then stir in the flour and nutmeg. Cook for 3–4 minutes, stirring constantly, then add the milk all at once. Season with salt and pepper. Bring to a boil, stirring constantly. • Simmer for 10 minutes, stirring almost continuously, then remove from heat. • Filling: Melt the butter in a small frying pan and sauté the onion over low heat until translucent. • Increase the heat and sauté the veal, ham, and chicken until browned all over. • Pour in the wine and cook until evaporated. • Pour in the stock and season with salt and pepper. Use a wooden spoon to scrape off any residue that begins to stick to the bottom of the pan. • Add the 3 tablespoons of Béchamel and cook for 15 minutes, stirring often. • Remove from the heat and let cool to lukewarm. • Preheat the oven to 400°F/200°C/gas 6. • Butter a baking dish. • Transfer the meat sauce to a food processor or blender and chop finely. • Mix in the egg, Parmesan, and nutmeg. • Spread a small amount of filling onto the pasta rectangles and roll them up. • Lay the cannelloni in a single layer in the prepared baking dish. Cover with the Béchamel, meat sauce, and dot with the butter. • Bake for 15–20 minutes, or until the sauces are bubbling. • Let rest for 10 minutes before serving.

Serves 6; Preparation: 1 hour 30 minutes + time to make the pasta; Cooking: 2 hours; Level: 3

TIMBALLINI DI TAGLIOLINI

Baked tagliolini with meat sauce

Pasta
- 1 quantity plain fresh pasta dough (see chart on page 8)
- 2 tablespoons coarse sea salt (to cook the pasta)

Cream sauce
- 4 tablespoons butter
- 4 tablespoons all-purpose/plain flour
- 1^2/$_3$ cups/400 ml beef stock
- ^{1}/$_2$ cup/125 ml fresh cream
- 5 leaves Belgian endives, cut in thin strips and cooked for 2–3 minutes in hot butter
- 1 tablespoon Marsala wine
- salt and freshly ground white pepper to taste
- ^{3}/$_4$ cup/90 g freshly grated Parmesan cheese
- 1 quantity Meat sauce (see *Baked cannelloni*, page 69)

Prepare the tagliolini following the instructions on pages 9–11. • Cream sauce: Melt the butter in a medium saucepan, then add the flour and cook for 1 minute, stirring constantly. • Add the stock, cream, endives, and Marsala, and season with salt and pepper. Simmer for 15 minutes, stirring constantly. Remove from the heat and set aside to cool. • Place a large pan of water over high heat with the coarse sea salt. Cover and bring to a boil. • Preheat the oven to 350°F/180°C/gas 4. • Butter 6 small ovenproof dishes. • Cook the pasta in the pan of boiling water for 1–2 minutes. • Drain well and place in a large bowl. Dust with the Parmesan and pour in the cream sauce and the meat sauce. Stir carefully until well mixed. • Divide the pasta mixture evenly among the ovenproof dishes. • Place a large pan half filled with cold water in the oven and carefully place the small dishes in the large pan. Cook for 15 minutes. Serve hot.

Serves 6; Preparation: 35 minutes + time to make the pasta; Cooking: 1 hour 30 minutes; Level 2

CANNELLONI AI FUNGHI

Cannelloni with mushrooms

Pasta
- 1^1/$_4$ quantities plain fresh pasta dough (see chart on page 8)
- 2 tablespoons coarse sea salt (to cook the pasta)
- 2 tablespoons extra-virgin olive oil (to cook the pasta)

Meat sauce
- 2 tablespoons butter
- 1 small onion, finely chopped
- 2^1/$_2$ oz/75 g prosciutto/Parma ham, finely chopped
- 1 oz/30 g dried porcini mushrooms, soaked in milk for 2 hours, drained and finely chopped
- 8 oz/250 g ground/minced veal or beef
- 4 oz/125 g ground/minced chicken
- scant ^{1}/$_2$ cup/100 ml dry white wine
- scant ^{1}/$_2$ cup/100 ml stock

- ^{3}/$_4$ cup/90 g freshly grated Parmesan cheese
- 2 eggs
- freshly grated nutmeg to taste
- salt and freshly ground black pepper to taste

Béchamel sauce
- 5 tablespoons butter
- ^{1}/$_2$ cup/75 g all-purpose/plain flour
- pinch of freshly grated nutmeg
- 3 cups/750 ml milk
- salt and freshly ground white pepper to taste
- 6 tablespoons tomato sauce
- ^{3}/$_4$ cup/90 g freshly grated Parmesan cheese
- 1 tablespoon butter, cut up

Prepare the pasta dough following the instructions on pages 9–11. Set aside to rest for 30 minutes. • Meat sauce: Melt the butter in a skillet (frying pan) and sauté the onion and prosciutto for 15 minutes over medium heat. • Add the mushrooms and cook for 2 minutes. • Add the veal and chicken and cook over high heat for 10 minutes, stirring often, until well browned. • Pour in the wine and cook until evaporated. • Pour in the stock and cover and cook over low heat for 30 minutes. • Divide the pasta dough into 5 pieces. Roll it through the machine one notch at a time down to the thinnest setting. Let dry on a lightly floured cloth for 30 minutes. • Béchamel sauce: Melt the butter in a medium saucepan, then stir in the flour and nutmeg. Cook for 3–4 minutes, stirring constantly, then add the milk all at once. Season with salt and pepper. Bring to a boil, stirring constantly. • Simmer for 10 minutes, stirring almost continuously, then remove from heat. • When the meat sauce is cooked, stir in 2 tablespoons of the Béchamel. • Place a large pan of water over high heat with half the coarse sea salt and oil. Cover and bring to a boil. • Cut the pasta into 4 x 6-inch (10 x 14-cm) rectangles. • Blanch the rectangles of pasta as you would for lasagne, following the instructions on page 66. Drain each piece and place in a bowl of cold water with the coarse sea salt and oil. Drain again and place on a damp cloth. • Preheat the oven to 450°F/225°C/gas 7. • Butter 6 small rectangular ovenproof dishes. • Spread the pieces of pasta with the meat sauce. Roll the pasta up and place the rolls in the ovenproof dishes. Cover with Béchamel and 1 tablespoon of tomato sauce. Sprinkle each dish with Parmesan and chopped butter. • Bake for 15 minutes, or until the tops are golden brown. • Serve hot.

Serves 6; Preparation: 1 hour + time to make the pasta + 2 hours to soak mushrooms; Cooking: 1 hour 30 minutes; Level 2

Above: Baked tagliolini with meat sauce

Below: Cannelloni with mushrooms

PASTICCIO DI TAGLIATELLE VERDI
Baked spinach tagliatelle

Pasta
- 1 quantity colored (spinach) pasta dough (see chart on page 8)
- 2 tablespoons coarse sea salt (to cook the pasta)

Béchamel sauce
- 3 tablespoons butter
- $^1/_3$ cup/50 g all-purpose/plain flour
- pinch of freshly grated nutmeg
- $2^2/_3$ cups/650 ml milk
- salt and freshly ground white pepper to taste

Sauce
- 4 tablespoons butter, cut up
- $^1/_2$ cup/60 g prosciutto/Parma ham, finely chopped
- 2 oz/60 g dried mushrooms, soaked in warm water for 15 minutes
- salt and freshly ground white pepper to taste
- 4 tablespoons freshly grated Parmesan cheese

Prepare the tagliatelle following the instructions on pages 9–11. Shape into nests and let dry on a lightly floured cloth for 30 minutes. • Béchamel sauce: Melt the butter in a medium saucepan, then stir in the flour and nutmeg. Cook for 3–4 minutes, stirring constantly, then add the milk all at once. Season with salt and pepper. Bring to a boil, stirring constantly. • Simmer for 10 minutes, stirring almost continuously, then remove from the heat. • Sauce: Melt the butter in a large frying pan and sauté the prosciutto over low heat until crispy. • Drain the mushrooms, reserving the water. • Chop the mushrooms coarsely and add to the prosciutto. Cook over medium heat for 6–7 minutes, or until the mushrooms are tender, gradually adding the reserved water. • Season with salt and pepper. • Place a large pan of water over high heat with the coarse sea salt. Cover and bring to a boil. • Preheat the oven to 375°F/ 190°C/gas 5. • Butter a baking dish. • Cook the pasta in the pan of boiling water until very al dente, about 1–2 minutes. • Drain well and place in a large bowl. • Carefully stir in the sauce, almost all the Béchamel, and 3 tablespoons of Parmesan. Place in the baking dish and top with the remaining Béchamel and sprinkle with the remaining cheese. • Bake for 30–35 minutes, or until golden brown. Serve hot.

Serves 4–6; Preparation: 1 hour + time to make the pasta; Cooking: 45 minutes; Level 2

CROSTATINE DI TAGLIATELLE
Baked tagliatelle crostini

Pasta
- 1 quantity plain fresh pasta dough (see chart on page 8)
- 2 tablespoons coarse sea salt (to cook the pasta)

Filling
- 5 tablespoons butter, cut up
- $^1/_2$ cup/75 g all-purpose/plain flour
- pinch of freshly ground nutmeg
- 3 cups/750 ml milk
- salt and freshly ground white pepper to taste
- 8 oz/250 g Mozzarella cheese, cut in cubes
- 5 oz/150 g ham, cut in cubes
- $^3/_4$ cup/90 g freshly grated Parmesan cheese
- 1 large egg

Topping
- 2 tablespoons butter, cut up
- 4 tablespoons freshly grated Parmesan cheese

Prepare the tagliatelle following the instructions on pages 9–11. Shape the tagliatelle into nests and let dry on a lightly floured cloth for 30 minutes. • Place a large pan of water over high heat with the coarse sea salt. Cover and bring to a boil. • Filling: Melt the butter in a medium saucepan, then stir in the flour and nutmeg. Cook for 3–4 minutes, stirring constantly, then add the milk all at once. Season with salt and pepper. Bring to a boil, stirring constantly. • Simmer for 10 minutes, stirring almost continuously, then remove from heat. • Cook the pasta in the pan of boiling water until very al dente, about 1–2 minutes. • Drain well and place in a large bowl. • Carefully stir in the sauce, Mozzarella, ham, $^3/_4$ cup (90 g) of Parmesan, and the egg. Season with salt and pepper and stir until well mixed. • Line a baking sheet lined with aluminum foil. Spread with the filling to about $^2/_3$-inch (2-cm) thick. Let rest in a dry place for at least 4 hours, or until firm. • Preheat the oven to 400°F/200°C/ gas 6. • Use a cookie cutter or glass to cut the mixture into $2^1/_2$-inch (6-cm) disks. • Sprinkle a baking sheet with the bread crumbs or line it with waxed paper. • Place the disks of pasta on the prepared sheet and sprinkle with the chopped butter and 4 tablespoons of Parmesan. • Bake for 10 minutes, or until golden brown. Serve hot straight from the oven.

Serves 4–6; Preparation: 1 hour + time to make the pasta + 4 hours to rest; Cooking: 30 minutes; Level 2

Baked tagliatelle crostini

ROSETTE DI PASTA AL RAGÙ BIANCO DI TOTANI
Rosettes with squid sauce

Pasta
- 3/4 quantity plain fresh pasta dough (see chart on page 8)
- 2 tablespoons coarse sea salt
- 2 tablespoons extra-virgin olive oil (to cook the pasta)

Squid sauce
- 4 tablespoons extra-virgin olive oil
- 1 small carrot, cut in small cubes
- 1 small stalk celery, finely chopped
- 1 bunch mixed aromatic herbs (rosemary, sage, bay leaves)
- 1 lb/500 g flying squid, cleaned and chopped in small cubes
- 3 juniper berries, crushed
- 2 cloves garlic, lightly crushed
- 1 shallot, finely chopped
- 1 tablespoon all-purpose/plain flour
- 4 tablespoons dry white wine
- 2 tablespoons sherry
- scant 1 cup/200 ml water or Fish stock (see page 97)
- 2 tablespoons finely chopped parsley
- salt and freshly ground white pepper to taste

Onion sauce
- 2 tablespoons extra-virgin olive oil
- 2 large onions, sliced
- 1/3 cup/30 g all-purpose/plain flour
- 2/3 cup/150 ml milk
- 1/2 cup/125 ml water or Fish stock (see page 97)
- salt and freshly ground white pepper to taste
- 1 1/4 cups/150 g coarsely grated Provolone cheese

Prepare the pasta dough following the instructions on pages 9–11. Set aside to rest for 30 minutes. • Divide the dough into 5 pieces. Roll it through the machine one notch at a time down to the thinnest setting. Let dry on a lightly floured cloth for 30 minutes. • Place a large pan of water over high heat with half the coarse sea salt and oil. Cover and bring to a boil. • Cut the pasta into 6 x 8-inch (15 x 20-cm) rectangles. • Blanch the rectangles of pasta as you would for lasagne, following the instructions on page 66. Drain each piece and place in a bowl of cold water with the remaining coarse sea salt and oil. Drain again and place on a damp cloth. • Squid sauce: Heat the oil in a large skillet (frying pan) and sauté the carrot, celery, and aromatic herbs for 3–4 minutes. • Add the squid, juniper berries, garlic, and shallot and sauté over high heat for 5 minutes. • Add the flour and cook for 3 minutes more. • Pour in the wine and sherry and cook until evaporated. • Add the water or fish stock, parsley, salt, and pepper and cook until the squid is tender. • Spread half the squid sauce over the bottoms of 6 individual ovenproof dishes and let cool. • Onion sauce: Heat the oil in a large skillet and cook the onions over medium-low heat for 15 minutes, stirring often. • Add the flour and cook for 3 minutes. • Pour in

the milk and stock and bring to a boil. Season with salt and pepper and cook for 10 minutes. • Remove from the heat and let cool. • Preheat the oven to 400°F/200°C/gas 6. • Spread the rectangles of pasta with half the squid sauce and sprinkle with the Provolone. Roll them up to form cannelloni and cut into slices just over 1 inch (3 cm) thick. • Place the pieces spiral side up in the dishes. Spoon the remaining squid sauce and the onion sauce over the top. • Bake for 40 minutes, or until brown on top. • Serve hot.

Serves 6; Preparation: 1 hour 30 minutes + time to make the pasta; Cooking: 2 hours; Level 3

TAGLIOLINI AL CARTOCCIO
Baked pasta with leeks

Pasta
- 1 1/2 quantities plain fresh pasta dough (see chart on page 8)
- 2 tablespoons coarse sea salt (to cook the pasta)

Sauce
- 3 tablespoons butter
- 5 leeks, white parts only, thinly sliced
- 2 cups/500 ml Meat stock (see page 97)
- 6 tablespoons milk
- salt and freshly ground white pepper to taste
- 8 oz/250 g canned/tinned tuna (preserved in oil), drained and crumbled
- 5 tablespoons fresh cream
- few drops Worcestershire sauce
- 3/4 cup/90 g freshly grated Parmesan cheese
- 1 tablespoon finely chopped parsley

Prepare the tagliolini following the instructions on pages 9–11. Shape into nests and let dry on a lightly floured cloth for 30 minutes. • Place a large pan of water over high heat with the coarse sea salt. Cover and bring to a boil. • Preheat the oven to 450°F/225°C/gas 8. • Line 6 small ovenproof dishes with waxed paper. There should be enough paper overlapping the edges to enclose the pasta. • Sauce: Melt the butter in a large saucepan over low heat. Cook the leeks with the stock and milk for 15 minutes. Season with salt and pepper. • Add the tuna, cream, and Worcestershire sauce and cook for 5 minutes. Remove from the heat. • Cook the pasta in the pan of boiling water until al dente, about 1 minute. • Drain well and toss gently with the sauce. Add the Parmesan and mix well. • Spoon the mixture into the prepared dishes and sprinkle with the parsley. Close the waxed paper over the pasta, so that it is sealed inside. • Bake for 8–10 minutes. • Serve hot.

Serves 6; Preparation: 30 minutes + time to make the pasta; Cooking: 40 minutes; Level 2

Above: Baked pasta with leeks

Below: Rosettes with squid sauce

TRONCHETTI AI TOTANI

Baked squid spirals with orange cream sauce

Pasta
- 1 quantity colored (spinach) pasta dough (see chart on page 8)
- 2 tablespoons coarse sea salt (to cook the pasta)
- 2 tablespoons extra-virgin olive oil (to cook the pasta)

Filling
- 12 medium flying squid (total weight about 2 lb/1 kg)
- salt and freshly ground white pepper to taste
- 1 orange
- 2 tablespoons butter
- 4 tablespoons extra-virgin olive oil

Cream sauce
- $4^1/_2$ tablespoons butter
- $1/_2$ cup/75 g all-purpose/plain flour
- 2 cups/500 ml Fish stock (see page 97)
- scant 1 cup/200 ml fresh cream
- salt and freshly ground white pepper to taste

Prepare the spinach pasta dough following the instructions on pages 9–11. Set aside to rest for 30 minutes. Filling: Bring a small saucepan of water to a boil with 1 teaspoon of salt. • Clean the squid and remove the skins. Cut the tentacles into small chunks. Use a sharp knife to cut the bodies lengthwise, then open them out into rectangles. Make small cuts all along the edges of the rectangles with the knife. • Blanch the rectangles in the saucepan of boiling water one at a time for 5–10 seconds. Drain and trim the edges of each piece to make it as even a rectangle as possible. Chop the trimmings finely and set aside. • Divide the pasta dough into 5 pieces. Roll it through the machine one notch at a time down to the second thinnest setting. Let dry on a lightly floured cloth for 30 minutes, then cut into 4-inch (10-cm) squares. • Place a large pan of water over high heat with half the coarse sea salt and oil. Cover and bring to a boil. • Blanch the rectangles of pasta as you would for lasagne, following the instructions on page 66. Drain each piece and place in a bowl of cold water with the remaining coarse sea salt and oil. Drain again and place on a damp cloth. • Cream sauce: Melt the butter in a saucepan. Stir in the butter and cook for 1 minute, stirring constantly with a wooden spoon. Pour in the stock and cream. Season with salt and pepper and simmer for 15 minutes, stirring constantly. • Peel half the orange and cut the peel into tiny pieces. • Melt 2 tablespoons of butter in a large skillet (frying pan) and add the oil. • Add the squid tentacles and cook for 1 minute, then add the squid trimmings. Season with salt and pepper and cook over high heat for 2 minutes. • Add the chopped orange peel and remove from heat. • Spread each sheet of pasta with a thin layer of cream sauce and cover each piece with a rectangle of squid. Spread each one with 1 tablespoon of the tentacle and orange mixture. • Carefully roll up each piece of pasta and wrap in plastic wrap (cling film). Refrigerate for at least 30 minutes. • Preheat the oven to 350°F/180°C/gas 4. • Butter 4 small individual ovenproof dishes. Spread the remaining cream evenly over the bottoms of the dishes. • Unwrap the pasta and squid rolls and use a sharp knife to slice each one into $3/_4$-inch (2-cm) pieces. Place the pieces, spiral side up, in the four dishes. • Bake for 15 minutes. • Serve hot.

Serves 4; Preparation: 1 hour 30 minutes + time to make the pasta + 30 minutes to chill; Cooking: 1 hour; Level 3

Baked squid spirals with orange cream sauce

LASAGNE ALLO STRACCHINO
Lasagne with fresh creamy cheese

Pasta
- $^3/_4$ quantity plain fresh pasta dough (see chart on page 8)
- 2 tablespoons coarse sea salt (to cook the pasta)
- 2 tablespoons extra-virgin olive oil (to cook the pasta)

Filling
- 7 oz/200 g nettles (tender tops only)
- 10 oz/300 g Swiss chard leaves (tough stalks removed)
- 10 oz/300 g watercress, cleaned
- salt and freshly ground white pepper to taste
- $^1/_2$ cup/125 ml extra-virgin olive oil
- 3 scallions/spring onions, finely chopped
- 10 oz/300 g zucchini/courgettes, cut in julienne (matchsticks), blanched for 1 minute
- 1 egg
- 14 oz/400 g Stracchino or other fresh creamy cheese
- $1^2/_3$ cups/400 ml milk
- pinch of freshly grated nutmeg
- 15 zucchini/courgette flowers, cleaned and cut in strips
- 1 tablespoon finely chopped parsley
- 1 tablespoon finely chopped marjoram
- $^1/_2$ cup/60 g freshly grated Parmesan cheese
- 2 tablespoons butter, cut up

Prepare the lasagne following the instructions on pages 9–11. • Place a large pan of water over high heat with half the coarse sea salt and oil. Cover and bring to a boil. • Blanch the sheets of lasagne following the instructions on page 66. • Preheat the oven to 400°F/200°C/gas 6. • Butter an ovenproof dish measuring about 8 x 12 inches (20 x 30 cm). • Filling: Place the nettles, Swiss chard, and watercress in a large pan with a pinch of salt and a scant $^1/_2$ cup (100 ml) of water. Cook over high heat for 10 minutes, or until the greens have released their cooking liquids and become tender. Drain well and chop them coarsely. • Heat 4 tablespoons of oil in a large skillet (frying pan) and sauté the scallions for 3 minutes. Add the zucchini and sauté for 4 minutes. • Beat the egg in a medium bowl and stir in the Stracchino. Pour in the milk and season with salt, pepper, and nutmeg. • Line the ovenproof dish with a layer of pasta. Cover with one-third of the greens, one-third of the zucchini flowers, and one-third of the zucchini mixture. Spread with a quarter of the cheese sauce and sprinkle with parsley, marjoram, and Parmesan. Repeat this layering process until all the ingredients are in the dish, finishing with a layer of cheese sauce and Parmesan. Dot with the butter. • Bake for 20 minutes, or until pale golden brown to top. • Let stand for 15 minutes before serving.

Serves 6; Preparation: 50 minutes + time to make the pasta; Cooking: 1 hour 30 minutes; Level 3

LASAGNE AL PESTO
Lasagne with basil sauce

Pasta
- $^3/_4$ quantity plain fresh pasta (see chart on page 8)
- 2 tablespoons coarse sea salt (to cook the pasta)
- 2 tablespoons extra-virgin olive oil (to cook the pasta)

Béchamel sauce
- 5 tablespoons butter
- $^1/_2$ cup/75 g all-purpose/plain flour
- pinch of freshly grated nutmeg
- 1 quart/1 liter milk
- salt and freshly ground white pepper to taste

Basil sauce
- 3–4 bunches basil (with small leaves)
- 1 clove garlic
- $^3/_4$ cup/90 g freshly grated Parmesan cheese
- 2 tablespoons freshly grated Pecorino romano cheese
- 2 walnuts, shelled
- 3 tablespoons pine nuts
- $^3/_4$ cup/180 ml extra-virgin olive oil (preferably from Liguria)
- 1 teaspoon coarse sea salt

Prepare the lasagne following the instructions on pages 9–11. • Place a large pan of water over high heat with the coarse sea salt and oil. Cover and bring to a boil. • Blanch the sheets of lasagne following the instructions on page 66. • Preheat the oven to 400°F/200°C/gas 6. • Butter an ovenproof dish measuring about 8 x 12 inches (20 x 30 cm). • Béchamel sauce: Melt the butter in a medium saucepan over medium heat, then stir in the flour and nutmeg. Cook for 1–2 minutes, stirring constantly, then add the milk all at once. Season with salt and pepper. Bring to a boil, stirring constantly. • Simmer for 10 minutes, stirring almost continuously, then remove from heat. • Basil sauce: Place the basil, garlic, 2 tablespoons of Parmesan, the Pecorino, walnuts, pine nuts, oil, and salt in a food processor and chop until smooth and creamy. • Line the ovenproof dish with a layer of pasta. Cover with a layer of Béchamel, basil sauce, and remaining Parmesan. Top with a layer of pasta. Repeat these layers until all the ingredients are in the dish. • Bake for 20 minutes, or until a light crust has formed on the top. • Let stand for 10 minutes before serving.

Serves 6; Preparation: 1 hour + time to make the pasta; Cooking: 40 minutes; Level 2

LASAGNE ALLA ZUCCA E TARTUFO
Lasagne with pumpkin and truffles

Pasta
- 1 quantity plain fresh pasta dough (see chart on page 8)
- 2 tablespoons coarse sea salt (to cook the pasta)
- 2 tablespoons extra-virgin olive oil (to cook the pasta)

Meat sauce
- 4 tablespoons extra-virgin olive oil
- 1 onion, finely chopped
- 14 oz/400 g guinea fowl (or chicken), boned and cut into very small chunks
- $3^{1}/_{2}$ oz/100 g prosciutto/Parma ham, cut in julienne strips (matchsticks)
- 4 tablespoons dry Marsala wine
- salt and freshly ground black pepper to taste
- about $1^{1}/_{3}$ cups/300 ml meat stock (see page 97)

Sauce
- 2 tablespoons dry Marsala wine
- 2 tablespoons balsamic vinegar
- 2 tablespoons butter
- 2 tablespoons all-purpose/plain flour
- $1^{1}/_{4}$ cups/310 ml fresh cream
- $1^{2}/_{3}$ cups/400 ml chicken stock
- pinch of freshly grated nutmeg
- salt and freshly ground white pepper to taste
- $^{3}/_{4}$ cup/90 g freshly grated Parmesan cheese

Filling
- 6 tablespoons extra-virgin olive oil
- 1 lb/500 g chanterelle (or a mixture of dried porcini and champignons) mushrooms, cleaned
- salt to taste
- 2 tablespoons finely chopped parsley
- 2 lb/1 kg winter squash/pumpkin, peeled, cut in small cubes, and baked in the oven until tender
- $^{2}/_{3}$ oz/20 g black truffles, in shavings

Prepare the lasagne following the instructions on pages 9–11. • Place a large pan of water over high heat with half the coarse sea salt and oil. Cover and bring to a boil. • Blanch the sheets of lasagne following the instructions on page 66. • Preheat the oven to 400°F/200°C/gas 6. • Butter an ovenproof dish measuring about 10 x 14 inches (25 x 35 cm). • Meat sauce: Heat the oil in a medium saucepan and sauté the onion until transparent. • Add the guinea fowl meat and cook until browned all over. • Stir in the prosciutto and cook until the fat is transparent. • Stir in the Marsala and cook until evaporated. Season with salt and pepper. Pour in the stock and simmer over low heat for 30 minutes. • Sauce: Place the Marsala and balsamic vinegar in a small saucepan and cook over low heat until reduced by half. • Melt the butter in a medium saucepan and stir in the flour. Cook for 1–2 minutes, stirring constantly. • Pour in the cream and stock. Season with the nutmeg, salt, and pepper. Bring to a boil and cook over very low heat for 15 minutes. • Stir in the Parmesan and the reduced vinegar and Marsala mixture. • Filling: Heat half the oil in a large skillet (frying pan) and sauté the mushrooms over medium heat until tender. Season with salt and add the parsley. • In a separate pan, heat the remaining oil and sauté the pumpkin over medium heat until tender. • Line the ovenproof dish with a layer of pasta. Cover with meat sauce, mushrooms, and sauce. Cover with another layer of pasta and spread with pumpkin and sauce and sprinkle with truffles. Repeat this layering process until all the ingredients are in the dish. • Bake for 20 minutes, or until pale golden brown to top. • Let stand for 15 minutes before serving.

Serves 6–8; Preparation: 1 hour + time to make the pasta; Cooking: 2 hours; Level 2

LASAGNE AL PREZZEMOLO
Parsley-patterned lasagne with mushrooms and cheese

The pretty parsley patterns on this lasagne make it an especially attractive dish. Be sure to place the six parsley-patterned sheets on the top of the lasagne. They should also be evenly spaced so that all six portions are decorated with parsley.

Pasta
- $3/4$ quantity plain fresh pasta dough (see chart on page 8)
- 6 large leaves flat-leaf parsley, in good condition, washed but still damp
- 2 tablespoons coarse sea salt (to cook the pasta)
- 1 tablespoon extra-virgin olive oil (to cook the pasta)

Filling
- $1 1/2$ lb/750 g mushrooms (porcini or white mushrooms)
- $1/2$ cup/125 ml extra-virgin olive oil
- salt and freshly ground white pepper to taste
- 7 tablespoons butter
- $2/3$ cup/100 g all-purpose/plain flour
- pinch of freshly grated nutmeg
- $1 1/2$ quarts/1.5 liters milk
- $3/4$ cup/90 g freshly grated Parmesan cheese
- 7 oz/200 g ham
- 7 oz/200 g cheese (Fontina, Edam, or similar), thinly sliced

Prepare the lasagne following the instructions on pages 9–11. Roll 2 sheets of pasta with the parsley in between, following the instructions on page 67. Cut this sheet in 6 pieces. • Place a large pan of water over high heat with half the coarse sea salt and oil. Cover and bring to a boil. • Blanch the sheets of lasagne following the instructions on page 66. Place the parsley-patterned pieces to one side. They should go on the top of the lasagne so that the pattern remains visible. • Filling: Clean the mushrooms and separate the stalks from the heads. Chop the stalks into cubes and the heads into slices about $1/2$ inch (1 cm) thick. • Heat 4 tablespoons of oil in a large skillet (frying pan) over high heat and cook the mushroom heads for 4 minutes. Remove from the pan and set aside. • Heat 2 tablespoons of oil in the same pan and add the stalks and a pinch of salt. Cover and cook over medium heat for 10 minutes, or until tender. • Melt 6 tablespoons of the butter in a medium saucepan over medium heat, then stir in the flour and nutmeg. Cook for 1–2 minutes, stirring constantly, then add the milk all at once. Season with salt and pepper. Bring to a boil, stirring constantly. • Simmer for 10 minutes, stirring almost continuously, then remove from the heat. • Stir the Parmesan into the sauce. • Chop the mushroom stalks and two-thirds of the sauce in a food processor. • Preheat the oven to 400°F/200°C/gas 6. • Butter an ovenproof dish measuring about 10 x 14 inches (25 x 35 cm). • Use a quarter of the plain (without parsley pattern) pasta sheets to line the ovenproof dish. Cover with one-third of the ham, one-third of the thinly sliced cheese, one-third of the sliced mushrooms, and one-third of the sauce with mushrooms. Repeat these layers twice and top with the remaining sheets of plain pasta. Spread with the plain sauce (without mushrooms) and cover this with the parsley-patterned sheets of pasta. • Chop the remaining butter and sprinkle over the top. Cover the dish with a sheet of aluminum and bake for 30 minutes. • Remove from the oven and let stand for 20 minutes before serving.

Serves 6; Preparation: 1 hour + time to make the pasta; Cooking: 1 hour 30 minutes; Level 3

Parsley-patterned lasagne with mushrooms and cheese

LASAGNE ALLE VERDURE DI PRIMAVERA
Lasagne with spring vegetables

Pasta
- $3/4$ quantity plain fresh pasta dough (see chart on page 8)
- 2 tablespoons coarse sea salt (to cook the pasta)
- 2 tablespoons extra-virgin olive oil (to cook the pasta)

Béchamel sauce
- $3^1/2$ oz/100 g butter
- $2/3$ cup/100 g all-purpose/plain flour
- pinch of freshly grated nutmeg
- $1^1/2$ quarts/1.5 liters milk
- salt and freshly ground white pepper to taste

Filling
- 5 tablespoons basil sauce (see *Lasagne with basil sauce,* page 78)
- 2 lb/1 kg ripe tomatoes, peeled, seeds removed, and coarsely chopped
- 1 lb/500 g potatoes, boiled and cut in cubes
- 14 oz/400 g green beans, boiled in lightly salted water and cut in short pieces
- 10 oz/300 g Mozzarella cheese, sliced
- $3/4$ cup/90 g freshly grated Parmesan cheese
- salt to taste

Prepare the lasagne following the instructions on pages 9–11. • Place a large pan of water over high heat with half the coarse sea salt and oil. Cover and bring to a boil. • Blanch the sheets of lasagne following the instructions on page 66. • Preheat the oven to 350°F/180°C/gas 4. • Butter an ovenproof dish measuring about 8 x 12 inches (20 x 30 cm). • Béchamel sauce: Melt the butter in a small saucepan over medium heat, then stir in the flour and nutmeg. Cook for 1–2 minutes, stirring constantly, then add the milk all at once. Season with salt and pepper. Bring to a boil, stirring constantly. • Simmer for 8–10 minutes, stirring almost continuously, then remove from heat. Set aside to cool. • Filling: Stir the basil sauce into the cooled Béchamel sauce. • Mix the tomatoes, potatoes, green beans, and Mozzarella in a large bowl. • Cover the bottom of the ovenproof dish with a layer of the mixed Béchamel and basil sauce. Cover with a layer of pasta followed by a layer of vegetables and Mozzarella. Season with salt and pepper and sprinkle with Parmesan. Repeat this layering process until all the ingredients are in the pan, finishing with a layer of Béchamel and Parmesan. • Bake for 45 minutes, or until golden brown on top. • Let stand for 15 minutes before serving.

Serves 4–6; Preparation: 1 hour + time to make the pasta; Cooking: 2 hours; Level 2

LASAGNE IN COCOTTE
Small baked lasagne

Pasta
- $1/2$ quantity plain fresh pasta dough (see chart on page 8)
- 1 quantity colored (spinach) pasta dough (see chart on page 8)
- 4 tablespoons coarse sea salt (to cook the pasta)
- 2 tablespoons extra-virgin olive oil (to cook the pasta)

Béchamel sauce
- 3 tablespoons butter
- scant $1/3$ cup/45 g all-purpose/plain flour
- 2 cups/500 ml milk
- pinch of freshly ground nutmeg
- salt and freshly ground white pepper to taste
- $3/4$ cup/180 ml Meat sauce (store-bought or see recipe, page 00)
- $3^1/2$ oz/100 g ham, cut in small cubes
- 6 tablespoons butter (4 tablespoons melted, 2 tablespoons cold, cut up)
- $1/2$ cup/60 g freshly grated Parmesan cheese
- salt to taste

Prepare the plain fresh pasta following the instructions on pages 9–11. Cut into 6 sheets measuring about 6 inches (15 cm) square and let dry on a lightly floured cloth for 30 minutes. • Prepare the spinach pasta following the instructions on pages 9–11, and 17. Cut into tagliolini and let dry on a lightly floured cloth for 30 minutes. • Place a large pan of water over high heat with 1 tablespoon of the coarse sea salt and half the oil. Cover and bring to a boil. • Blanch the sheets of lasagne following the instructions on page 66. • Place a second large pan of water over high heat with the remaining coarse sea salt. Cover and bring to a boil. • Butter 6 ovenproof dishes (about 4 inches/10 cm in diameter) and line each one with a sheet of lasagne. Leave the extra pieces of pasta overlapping the edges. • Béchamel sauce: Melt the butter in a medium saucepan, then stir in the flour and nutmeg. Cook for 1–2 minutes, stirring constantly, then add the milk all at once. Season with salt and pepper. Bring to a boil, stirring constantly. • Simmer for 10 minutes, stirring almost continuously, then remove from the heat. • Preheat the oven to 400°F/200°C/gas 6. • Cook the spinach tagliolini in the pan of boiling water until very al dente, about 1–2 minutes. • Drain well and place in a large bowl. • Add the Béchamel, meat sauce, ham, and melted butter and toss gently. • Divide the tagliolini equally among the 6 ovenproof dishes and sprinkle with the Parmesan and cold butter. Fold the pieces of overlapping pasta over the top so that the tagliolini are almost covered. • Bake for 10 minutes, or until golden brown on top. • Serve hot.

Serves 6; Preparation: 45 minutes + time to make the pasta; Cooking: 1 hour; Level 2

Small baked lasagne

LASAGNE AL RADICCHIO
Radicchio lasagne

Pasta
- $^3/_4$ quantity plain fresh pasta dough (see chart on page 8)
- 2 tablespoons coarse sea salt (to cook the pasta)
- 2 tablespoons extra-virgin olive oil (to cook the pasta)

Filling
- 1 oz/30 g dried porcini mushrooms, soaked for 2 hours in water (at room temperature)
- 2 tablespoons butter
- 1 small onion, finely chopped
- salt and freshly ground black pepper to taste
- 1 lb/500 g Chioggia or green radicchio, finely chopped
- $^1/_2$ cup/125 ml dry Marsala wine
- $^1/_2$ cup/60 g freshly grated Parmesan cheese
- $^1/_2$ cup/60 g freshly grated Fontina cheese
- 2 large egg yolks

Béchamel sauce
- 5 tablespoons butter
- $^1/_2$ cup/75 g all-purpose/plain flour
- pinch of freshly grated nutmeg
- $3^1/_4$ cups/800 ml milk
- salt and freshly ground white pepper to taste

Topping
- 3 tablespoons butter, cut up
- 4 tablespoons freshly grated Parmesan cheese

Prepare the lasagne following the instructions on pages 9–11. • Place a large pan of water over high heat with half the coarse sea salt and oil. Cover and bring to a boil. • Blanch the sheets of lasagne following the instructions on page 66. • Filling: Drain the mushrooms and chop them finely. • Heat the 2 tablespoons of butter in a large saucepan and add the onion and mushrooms. Season with salt. Cover and cook over low heat for 15 minutes. • Add the radicchio. Season with salt, and cover and cook over medium heat for 10 minutes. • Pour in the Marsala and cook until evaporated. • Cook for 5 minutes. Remove from the heat and let cool a little. • Béchamel sauce: Melt the butter in a medium saucepan, then stir in the flour and nutmeg. Cook for 3–4 minutes, stirring constantly, then add the milk all at once. Season with salt and pepper. Bring to a boil, stirring constantly. • Simmer for 10 minutes, stirring almost continuously, then remove from heat. • Stir the Parmesan, Fontina, and egg yolks into the Béchamel. Season with salt and pepper. • Preheat the oven to 400°F/200°C/gas 6. • Butter an ovenproof dish measuring about 10 x 14 inches (25 x 35 cm). • Cover the bottom and sides with a layer of lasagne sheets. Leave enough pasta hanging over the edges to fold over the lasagne in the pan. Spoon in a third of the radicchio mixture and cover with another layer of pasta. Spoon another third of the radicchio mixture over the top and then fold the overhanging pieces of pasta over the filling. Cover with another layer of pasta and the remaining radicchio mixture. • Topping: Dot with the butter and sprinkle with the Parmesan. • Bake for about 40 minutes, or until the top is golden brown. • Let rest for 20 minutes before serving.

Serves 6–8; Preparation: 50 minutes + time to make the pasta; Cooking: 1 hour 30 minutes; Level 2

SFORMATINI DI PASTA CON VERDURA
Baked pasta molds with vegetables

Pasta
- $^1/_2$ quantity plain fresh pasta dough (see chart on page 8)
- $^1/_2$ quantity colored (spinach) pasta dough (see chart on page 8)
- 2 tablespoons coarse sea salt (to cook the pasta)

Cream sauce
- 5 tablespoons butter
- $^1/_2$ cup/75 g all-purpose/plain flour
- $1^1/_4$ cups/310 ml Meat stock (see page 97)
- $1^2/_3$ cups/400 ml fresh cream
- salt and freshly ground white pepper to taste

Filling
- 10 oz/300 g mixed vegetables, cut in small cubes (a mix of peas, carrots, and green beans is ideal)
- 6 tablespoons butter
- salt and freshly ground white pepper to taste
- $^3/_4$ cup/90 g freshly grated Pecorino cheese
- 1 large egg

Prepare both types of pasta dough following the instructions on pages 9–11, and 17. Cut into taglierini and shape into nests. Let dry on a lightly floured cloth for 30 minutes. • Place a large pan of water over high heat with the coarse sea salt. Cover and bring to a boil. • Preheat the oven to 350°F/180°C/gas 4. • Cream sauce: Melt the 5 tablespoons of butter in a medium saucepan and add the flour. Cook for 1 minute, stirring constantly. Pour in the stock and cream. Season with salt and pepper. Bring to a boil and simmer for 15 minutes, stirring constantly. • Filling: Cook the vegetables in salted, boiling water for 5 minutes. • Drain and place in a bowl of cold water to cool. • Melt 3 tablespoons of butter in a large skillet (frying pan). Drain the vegetables thoroughly and add to the skillet. Cook for 5 minutes over low heat. Season with salt and pepper and remove from the heat. • Cook the pasta in the pan of boiling water until al dente, about 1 minute. • Drain well and toss with the remaining butter. • Cover the bottom of each of 8 small ovenproof dishes with a layer of pasta. • Mix the remaining pasta into the cream sauce. Add the vegetables, Pecorino, and egg. Mix well, then divide evenly among the ovenproof dishes. • Bake for about 30 minutes, or until golden brown. • Turn each dish out onto an individual serving plate and serve hot.

Serves 8; Preparation: 1 hour + time to make the pasta; Cooking: 1 hour; Level 3

Above: Baked pasta molds with vegetables

Below: Radicchio lasagne

LASAGNE DI FARINA DI CECI E VERDURE ESTIVE

Garbanzo bean lasagne with summer vegetables

Pasta
- 1 cup/150 g garbanzo bean/chickpea flour
- 1 cup/150 g all-purpose/plain flour
- 3 very fresh large eggs
- 2 tablespoons coarse sea salt (to cook the pasta)
- 2 tablespoons extra-virgin olive oil (to cook the pasta)

Filling
- 4 oz/125 g green beans, cut in short lengths
- 6 tablespoons extra-virgin olive oil
- 1 onion, finely chopped
- 1 lb/500 g zucchini/courgettes, cut in small cubes
- 10 oz/300 g carrots, cut in small cubes
- 1 red bell pepper/capsicum, cut in small squares
- salt and freshly ground white pepper to taste
- scant 1 cup/200 ml fresh cream
- 1 lb/500 g fresh Ricotta cheese, drained
- 3/4 cup/90 g freshly grated Parmesan cheese

Pasta: Sift both flours onto a clean work surface and gradually stir in the eggs using a fork. Follow the instructions on pages 9–11 to mix the dough, then knead for 20 minutes. Wrap the dough in plastic wrap (cling film) and let rest for 30 minutes. • Place a large pan of water over high heat with half the coarse sea salt and oil. Cover and bring to a boil. • Divide the dough into 5 pieces. Roll it through the machine one notch at a time down to the thinnest setting. Cut the pasta with a knife into rectangles about 4 x 6 inches (10 x 15 cm). Let dry on a lightly floured cloth for 30 minutes. • Blanch the sheets of lasagne following the instructions on page 66. • Preheat the oven to 350°F/180°C/gas 4. • Butter an ovenproof dish measuring about 8 x 12 inches (20 x 30 cm). • Blanch the beans in salted, boiling water for 2–3 minutes. Drain well. • Heat the oil in a large skillet (frying pan) and sauté the onion for 5 minutes. • Add the zucchini, carrots, bell pepper, and beans. Season with salt and sauté over high heat for about 8 minutes. • Pour in the cream and bring to a boil. Cook for 1–2 minutes, then remove from the heat. • Place the Ricotta in a large bowl and season with salt and pepper. • Cover the bottom of the ovenproof dish with a layer of pasta. Spread with a layer of Ricotta and cover with a layer of vegetables. Sprinkle with the Parmesan. Repeat this layering process until all the ingredients are in the dish, finishing with a layer of vegetables and Parmesan. • Bake for 30 minutes, or until golden brown on top. • Let stand for 15 minutes before serving.

Serves 6; Preparation: 1 hour + time to make the pasta; Cooking: 1 hour; Level 2

LASAGNE E VERZA

Cabbage lasagne

- 1/2 quantity plain fresh pasta (see chart on page 8)
- 2 tablespoons coarse sea salt (to cook the pasta)
- 1 tablespoon extra-virgin olive oil (to cook the pasta)

Béchamel sauce
- 1 1/2 tablespoons butter
- 2 tablespoons all-purpose/plain flour
- pinch of freshly grated nutmeg
- 1 1/4 cups/310 ml milk
- salt and freshly ground white pepper to taste

Filling
- 6 large cabbage leaves
- 3 1/2 oz/100 g Edam cheese (or similar), thinly sliced
- 3 oz/90 g ham, thinly sliced
- 4 tablespoons butter, cut up
- 1/2 cup/60 g freshly grated Parmesan cheese
- 3 tablespoons milk
- 4 tablespoons fresh cream
- salt to taste

Prepare the lasagne following the instructions on pages 9–11. • Place a large pan of water over high heat with half the coarse sea salt and oil. Cover and bring to a boil. • Blanch the sheets of lasagne following the instructions on page 66. • Preheat the oven to 350°F/180°C/gas 4. • Butter an ovenproof dish measuring about 6 x 8 inches (15 x 20 cm). • Béchamel sauce: Melt the butter in a small saucepan over medium heat, then stir in the flour and nutmeg. Cook for 1–2 minutes, stirring constantly, then add the milk all at once. Season with salt and pepper. Bring to a boil, stirring constantly. • Simmer for 8–10 minutes, stirring almost continuously, then remove from heat. • Filling: Blanch the cabbage leaves in a large saucepan of salted, boiling water for 1–2 minutes. Drain well. • Line the ovenproof dish with a layer of pasta. Cover with 2 cabbage leaves, one-third of the thinly sliced cheese, one-third of the ham, and one-third of the Béchamel. Dot with a little butter and sprinkle with a little Parmesan. Repeat these layers twice and top with the remaining sheets of pasta. • Mix the milk and cream together in a small bowl and drizzle over the lasagne. • Bake for 30 minutes, or until pale golden brown on top. • Let stand for 15 minutes before serving.

Serves 4; Preparation: 30 minutes + time to make the pasta; Cooking: 45 minutes; Level 2

LASAGNE DI PESCE
Seafood lasagne

Pasta
- $3/4$ quantity plain fresh pasta dough (see chart on page 8)
- 2 tablespoons coarse sea salt (to cook the pasta)
- 2 tablespoons extra-virgin olive oil (to cook the pasta)

Filling
- 4 tablespoons extra-virgin olive oil
- 2 cloves garlic, finely chopped
- 2 tablespoons finely chopped parsley
- $1/2$ cup/125 ml dry white wine
- 10 oz/300 g shrimps, peeled
- 12 oz/350 g mixed clams, mussels, and scallops, shelled
- 1 small white firm-textured fish (weighing about 14 oz/400 g), cleaned
- 10 oz/300 g chopped squid

Fish sauce
- 6 tablespoons butter, cut up
- $1/2$ cup/75 g all-purpose/plain flour
- salt and freshly ground white pepper to taste
- 1 quart/1 liter Fish stock (see page 97)

Prepare the lasagne following the instructions on pages 9–11. • Place a large pan of water over high heat with half the coarse sea salt and oil. Cover and bring to a boil. • Filling: Heat the oil in a large skillet (frying pan) and sauté the garlic and half the parsley for 3 minutes. • Add the wine and cook until evaporated. • Add the shrimps, mixed shellfish, fish, and squid. Season with salt and pepper and cook over medium heat for 10 minutes. Add the remaining parsley just before removing from the heat. • Cook the sheets of lasagne in the boiling water following the instructions on page 66. • Preheat the oven to 350°F/180°C/gas 4. • Butter an ovenproof dish measuring about 8 x 12 inches (20 x 30 cm). • Fish sauce: Melt the butter in a medium saucepan and stir in the flour. Pour in the stock and simmer for 10 minutes, stirring almost constantly. • Cover the bottom of the ovenproof dish with a layer of pasta. Spread with a layer of fish sauce and cover with a layer of filling. Repeat this layering process until all the ingredients are in the dish. • Bake for 20 minutes, or until golden brown on top. • Let stand for 10 minutes before serving.

Serves 4–6; Preparation: 50 minutes + time to make the pasta; Cooking: 1 hour; Level 2

LASAGNE AI FUNGHI MISTI
Mushroom lasagne

Pasta
- $3/4$ quantity plain fresh pasta dough (see chart on page 8)
- 2 tablespoons coarse sea salt (to cook the pasta)
- 2 tablespoons extra-virgin olive oil (to cook the pasta)

Filling
- $2^1/2$ lb/1.2 kg mixed mushrooms
- 4 tablespoons extra-virgin olive oil
- 2 cloves garlic, finely chopped
- 1 sprig fresh rosemary
- salt and freshly ground white pepper to taste
- 2 tablespoons finely chopped parsley
- $1^1/2$ lb/750 g Mascarpone cheese
- 6 large egg yolks
- 1 cup/125 g freshly grated Parmesan cheese

Prepare the lasagne following the instructions on pages 9–11. • Place a large pan of water over high heat with half the coarse sea salt and oil. Cover and bring to a boil. • Blanch the sheets of lasagne following the instructions on page 66. • Filling: Clean the mushrooms carefully, removing any dirt from the stems with a sharp knife and wiping well with a damp cloth. If necessary, run briefly under cold running water; but make sure they don't absorb water. Chop into $3/4$-inch (2-cm) cubes. • Heat the oil in a large skillet (frying pan) over high heat and sauté the garlic and rosemary for 2 minutes. • Add the mushrooms and cook for 5 minutes, or until all the water they release has evaporated. • Cover and cook over medium-low heat for 10 minutes, or until tender. Season with salt and pepper and remove from the heat. Stir in the parsley. • Preheat the oven to 350°F/180°C/ gas 4. • Butter an ovenproof dish measuring about 10 x 14 inches (25 x 35 cm). • Place the Mascarpone in a medium bowl and stir in the egg yolks and almost all the Parmesan. Season with salt and pepper. Refrigerate until ready to use. • Cover the bottom and sides of the ovenproof dish with a layer of lasagne sheets. Spoon in a quarter of the mushroom mixture followed by one-fifth of the Mascarpone mixture. Cover with another layer of pasta and repeat until there are four layers in the dish. Finish with the remaining Mascarpone and sprinkle with the remaining Parmesan. • Bake for about 30 minutes, or until the top is golden brown.

Serves 6–8; Preparation: 45 minutes + time to make the pasta; Cooking: 1 hour; Level 2

Mushroom lasagne

CANNELLONI VERDE ALLE VERDURE

Spinach cannelloni with vegetables

Pasta
- 1 quantity colored (spinach) pasta dough (see chart on page 8)
- 2 tablespoons coarse sea salt (to cook the pasta)
- 2 tablespoons extra-virgin olive oil (to cook the pasta)

Béchamel sauce
- 3 tablespoons butter
- $1/3$ cup/50 g all-purpose/plain flour
- pinch of freshly grated nutmeg
- $2^2/3$ cups/650 ml milk
- salt and freshly ground white pepper to taste

Filling
- 3 artichoke hearts, cleaned, sliced and soaked in cold water with lemon juice
- juice and finely grated zest of $1/2$ lemon
- 2 carrots, cut in matchsticks
- 2 zucchini/courgettes, cut in matchsticks
- $1/2$ teaspoon sugar
- 3 tablespoons butter
- 2 tablespoons extra-virgin olive oil
- 1 leek, white part only, sliced
- salt and freshly ground white pepper to taste
- 7 oz/200 g Stracchino cheese
- $1^1/4$ cups/150 g freshly grated Parmesan cheese

Prepare the spinach pasta dough following the instructions on pages 9–11. Set aside to rest for 30 minutes. • Divide the pasta dough into 5 pieces. Roll it through the machine one notch at a time down to the second thinnest setting. Let dry on a lightly floured cloth for 30 minutes. • Place a large pan of water over high heat with the coarse sea salt and oil. Cover and bring to a boil. • Béchamel sauce: Melt the butter in medium saucepan, then stir in the flour and nutmeg. Cook for 3–4 minutes, stirring constantly, then add the milk all at once. Season with salt and pepper. Bring to a boil, stirring constantly. • Simmer for 10 minutes, stirring almost continuously, then remove from heat. • Cut the pasta into 4-inch (10-cm) squares. • Blanch the squares of pasta as you would for lasagne, following the instructions on page 66. Drain each piece and place in a bowl of cold water with the remaining 1 tablespoon of oil. Drain again and place on a damp cloth sticking them together in pairs along the short sides. • Filling: Boil the artichoke hearts in salted water with lemon juice until just tender. Drain and set aside. • Boil the carrots and zucchini in salted water with the sugar until just tender. Drain and set aside. • Heat the butter and oil in a large skillet (frying pan) and sauté the leek with a little salt for 15 minutes. • Add the carrots and cook for 2 minutes. • Add the artichokes and cook for 2 more minutes. • Add the zucchini. Season with salt and cook over low heat for 5 more minutes. Remove from the heat and let cool. • Preheat the oven to 350°F/180°C/gas 4. • Butter 8 small ovenproof baking dishes and cover the bottoms with most of the Béchamel. • Mix the Stracchino, Parmesan, and lemon zest in a medium bowl. Stir in the artichokes, leek, carrots, and zucchini and season with salt and pepper. • Spread each piece of pasta with vegetable mixture and roll them up to form cannelloni. • Place the cannelloni in the dishes and cover with the remaining Béchamel. • Bake for 15 minutes, or until pale golden brown.

Serves 8: Preparation: 1 hour + time to make the pasta; Cooking: 1 hour; Level 2

TAGLIOLINI AL FORNO
Baked tagliolini

Pasta
- $^1/_2$ quantity plain fresh pasta dough (see chart on page 8)
- $^1/_2$ quantity colored (spinach) pasta dough (see chart on page 8)
- 2 tablespoons coarse sea salt (to cook the pasta)

Sauce
- 1 cauliflower, weighing about $1^1/_4$ lb/650 g
- 1 tablespoon white wine vinegar
- salt and freshly ground white pepper to taste
- $3^1/_2$ oz/100 g smoked Scamorza cheese, cut in $^1/_4$-inch/5-mm slices
- $3^1/_2$ oz/100 g smoked ham, cut in $^1/_4$-inch/5-mm dice
- 4 tablespoons butter, cut up
- $^1/_3$ cup/50 g all-purpose/plain flour
- 2 cups/500 ml milk
- pinch of nutmeg

Prepare the two types of tagliolini following the instructions on pages 9–11, and 17. • Sauce: Divide the cauliflower into small florets and cut the stalk into small cubes. • Heat enough water to cover the cauliflower in a medium saucepan. Add the vinegar, salt, and cauliflower stalks and cook for 5 minutes. • Add the florets and cook for 5–10 minutes more, or until the cauliflower is tender. • Drain well, reserving $^3/_4$ cup (200 ml) of the cooking water. Place the cauliflower in a bowl, cover with plastic wrap (cling film), and let cool. • Place a large pan of water over high heat with the coarse sea salt. Cover and bring to a boil. • Preheat the oven to 400°F/200°C/gas 6. • Butter an ovenproof dish measuring about 8 x 12 inches (20 x 30 cm). • Melt the butter in a medium saucepan. Add the flour and cook over medium heat for 3 minutes, stirring constantly. • Remove from the heat and pour in the milk and reserved cauliflower water. Return to the heat and beat vigorously with a wire whisk to prevent any lumps from forming. Bring to a boil and stir with a wooden spoon. Season with salt, pepper, and nutmeg. Cover and simmer over very low heat for 10 minutes, stirring often. • Mix the sauce and cauliflower in a bowl and let cool to room temperature. • Cook the pasta in the boiling water for 1 minute. • Drain well and carefully stir into the cauliflower mixture. • Cover the bottom of the baking dish with one-third of the tagliolini mixture and sprinkle with half the cheese and half the ham. Cover with another third of the tagliolini mixture, and sprinkle with the remaining cheese and ham. Cover with the remaining tagliolini mixture. • Bake for 10 minutes, or until golden brown on top. • Let stand for 5 minutes before serving.

Serves 4; Preparation: 45 minutes + time to make the pasta; Cooking: 1 hour; Level 2

ROSELLINE AI SALUMI
Pasta rolls with cheese and ham

Pasta
- $^3/_4$ quantity plain fresh pasta dough (see chart on page 8)
- 2 tablespoons coarse sea salt
- 2 tablespoons extra-virgin olive oil (to cook the pasta)

Béchamel sauce
- 2 tablespoons butter, cut up
- 2 tablespoons all-purpose/plain flour
- pinch of freshly grated nutmeg
- 2 cups/500 ml milk
- salt and freshly ground white pepper to taste

Filling
- 10 oz/300 g thinly sliced Edam cheese
- 5 oz/150 g thinly sliced mortadella
- 5 oz/150 g thinly sliced prosciutto/Parma ham
- $1^1/_2$ cups/180 g freshly grated Parmesan cheese

Prepare the pasta dough following the instructions on pages 9–11. Set aside to rest for 30 minutes. • Divide the pasta dough into 5 pieces. Roll it through the machine one notch at a time down to the thinnest setting. Let dry on a lightly floured cloth for 30 minutes. • Place a large pan of water over high heat with the coarse sea salt and oil. Cover and bring to a boil. • Béchamel sauce: Melt the butter in a medium saucepan, then stir in the flour and nutmeg. Cook for 3–4 minutes, stirring constantly, then add the milk all at once. Season with salt and pepper. Bring to a boil, stirring constantly. • Simmer for 10 minutes, stirring almost continuously, then remove from the heat. • Cut the pasta into 4 x 6-inch (10 x 14-cm) rectangles. • Blanch the rectangles of pasta as you would for lasagne, following the instructions on page 66. Drain each piece and place in a bowl of cold water with the remaining coarse sea salt and oil. Drain again and place on a damp cloth sticking them together in pairs along the short sides. • Preheat the oven to 350°F/180°C/gas 4. • Butter a large ovenproof baking dish and smear with a little of the Béchamel. • Filling: Cover the pasta with the slices of Edam and place slices of mortadella on half the pieces of pasta and slices of ham on the others. • Sprinkle with the Parmesan and roll the pasta up into loose rolls about 4 inches (10 cm) long. Cut each roll in half and place in the ovenproof dish. Spread the Béchamel over the top. • Bake for 20 minutes, or until nicely browned. • Serve hot.

Serves 6; Preparation: 1 hour 30 minutes + time to make the pasta; Cooking: 40 minutes; Level 3

NIDI DI TAGLIATELLE ALLA FONDUTA
Tagliatelle nests with cheese fondue

Pasta
- $1/2$ quantity plain fresh pasta dough (see chart on page 8)
- 2 tablespoons coarse sea salt (to cook the pasta)

Fondue
- 3 oz/90 g Fontina cheese, thinly sliced and soaked in $1/2$ cup/125 ml milk
- 5 oz/150 g Robiola cheese
- 3 tablespoons fresh cream
- 2 tablespoons milk
- 2 large egg yolks
- salt and freshly ground white pepper to taste
- 6 tablespoons butter, melted
- 4 tablespoons freshly grated Parmesan cheese
- salt and freshly ground white pepper to taste

Prepare the tagliatelle following the instructions on pages 9–11. Shape the tagliatelle into nests and let dry on a lightly floured cloth for 30 minutes. • Place a large pan of water over high heat with the coarse sea salt. Cover and bring to a boil. • Preheat the oven to 450°F/225°C/gas 8. • Fondue: Drain the Fontina from the milk, discarding the milk. Place in a medium, heavy-bottomed pan with the Robiola, cream, and 2 tablespoons of milk and cook over low heat until the cheese has melted. • Remove from the heat and beat in the egg yolks, one at a time. Season with salt and pepper. • Place the pan with the fondue in a larger pan of barely simmering water and keep warm. • Cook the pasta in the pan of boiling water until very al dente, about 3–4 minutes. • Drain well and toss with the melted butter, Parmesan, and a pinch of salt. • Divide the fondue among 4 small ovenproof dishes and top each one with a quarter of the tagliatelle mixture. • Bake for 5 minutes, or until pale golden brown. • Serve hot.

Serves 4: Preparation: 30 minutes + time to make the pasta; Cooking: 30 minutes; Level 2

TORTA DI TAGLIATELLE
Tagliatelle cake

This is the only sweet dish in this book. The recipe comes from Emilia-Romagna, in central Italy, where it is very popular. This version of the recipe was given to us by Sig.ra Carla Mingarelli.

Pasta
- $1/2$ quantity plain fresh pasta dough (see chart on page 8)
- 2 tablespoons coarse sea salt

Shortcrust pastry
- 2 cups/300 g all-purpose/plain flour
- $1/2$ cup/125 g cold butter, cut up
- $3/4$ cup/125 g confectioners'/icing sugar
- 3 large egg yolks
- finely grated zest of $1/2$ lemon
- pinch of salt

Filling
- 4 tablespoons golden raisins/sultanas
- 4 tablespoons pine nuts
- 3 tablespoons candied citron peel, cut in small cubes
- 3 tablespoons rum or brandy
- 3 large egg yolks
- 6 tablespoons sugar
- 2–3 tablespoons milk or cream
- salt to taste

Prepare the tagliatelle following the instructions on pages 9–11. Shape the tagliatelle into nests and place on a lightly flour cloth until ready to use. • Shortcrust pastry: Sift the flour into a large bowl and add the butter confectioners' sugar, egg yolks, lemon zest, and salt. Mix rapidly with your hands and shape into a ball. Wrap in plastic wrap (cling film) and refrigerate for 30 minutes. • Place a large pan of water over high heat with the coarse sea salt. Cover and bring to a boil. • Preheat the oven to 400°F/200°C/gas 6. • Roll the pastry out on a lightly floured work surface. Place in an 8-inch (20-cm) round springform pan and prick well with the tines (prongs) of a fork. • Cover the pastry with aluminum foil and fill with dried beans. • Bake for 15–20 minutes, or until the edges are pale golden brown. Remove from the oven and let cool. Remove the beans and foil. • Filling: Soak the sultanas, pine nuts, and citron peel in a small bowl with the rum or brandy. • In a separate bowl, beat the egg yolks with the sugar until pale and creamy. Beat in the milk or cream. • Cook the tagliatelle in the boiling water for 2 minutes. Drain well and mix with the egg and sugar mixture and dried fruit. Mix well and spoon into the precooked pastry shell. • Bake for 30 minutes, or until the filling mixture is dried out. • Serve warm or cold.

Serves 6–8; Preparation: 1 hour + time to make the pasta; Cooking: 1 hour; Level 2

Above: Tagliatelle nests with cheese fondue

Below: Tagliatelle cake

Filled

Making filled pasta can be time consuming but your efforts are rewarded with exquisite dishes that can only be made at home. The first part of the process is the same as for simple fresh or baked pasta: you make the dough and roll it through the machine, then you prepare a filling and cut and fold the pasta to enclose it. In this chapter we have included some simpler recipes like *Anolini in beef stock* and *Potato and pumpkin ravioli*, as well as some virtuoso dishes, such as *Pasta sacks with zucchini* and *Braids with asparagus and Gorgonzola filling*.

Above: Ravioli with mushrooms (page 108)
Left: Pasta sacks with zucchini (page 102)

Half-moon ravioli and tortellini

Use a round pastry or cookie cutter to make half-moon shaped ravioli. With just a little extra folding these can become exquisite little tortellini ("little cakes") or slightly larger tortelloni. Tortelloni can be so large that you only need to serve 3 or 4 per person. Tortellini differ from cappelletti ("little hats," see page 99), because they have rounded rather than pointed edges.

see page 99

Fillings and sauces

Fillings can be made from any number of combinations of vegetables, cheese, meat, or seafood. The sauce should be chosen carefully so that it doesn't clash with or override the filling. Often a simple butter and herb sauce is sufficient.

❶
Roll the pasta dough into a thin sheet and place on a clean dry work surface. Use a smooth pastry or cookie cutter to cut out disks of pasta.

❷
Place a blob of filling at the center of each disk, then pick each one up and fold the pasta over to seal in a half-moon shape.

❸
To prepare tortellini or tortelli, continue by folding the edges of the half-moon pasta back on themselves.

❹
Finish by twisting the pasta around your index finger and sealing the ends.

❺
The first part of the sequence produces simple half-moon ravioli.

❻
The second part of the sequence produces tortellini, tortelli, or tortelloni (depending on their size; tortelloni being the largest).

Anolini

Anolini are small, round ravioli from Emilia-Romagna in central Italy. They are usually served in boiling meat stock (see our recipe on page 103), although they can also be served with sauces. Fillings are traditionally meat-based but they can also be made with vegetables, cheese, or seafood.

 Roll the pasta dough into a thin sheet and place on a clean dry work surface. Place blobs of filling at regular intervals on one half of the sheet, then fold the other half of the sheet over the top.

 Press down gently between the blobs of filling with your fingertips to remove excess air, then use a plain or fluted pastry or cookie cutter to cut out disks.

 Anolini are generally quite small, but you can make them any size you like. They can have smooth or fluted edges.

Fish stock

Ingredients
- 1 lb/500 g heads and bones mixed fish (sea bass, brill, sole, grouper, etc.)
- 3 quarts/3 liters cold water
- 1 carrot, chopped
- 1 stalk celery, chopped
- 1 onion, chopped
- 1 shallot, chopped
- 4 sprigs parsley
- 1 bay leaf
- 4 black peppercorns
- scant 1 cup/100 ml dry white wine
- 1 clove garlic
- 1 sprig thyme
- 1 tablespoon coarse sea salt

Soak the fish heads and bones in a large bowl of cold water for 1 hour. This will remove any residues of blood. Drain and place in a large saucepan with the water over low heat. Bring to a boil and simmer over low heat. Add all the other ingredients. Simmer for about 90 minutes. Drain the stock, filter, and use as indicated in the recipes. This stock will keep 4–5 days in the refrigerator or up to 3 months in the freezer.
Makes: 2 quarts/2 liters

Meat stock

Ingredients
- 1 medium boiling chicken, cleaned
- 1 lb/500 g boiling beef
- 4 quarts/4 liters cold water
- 1 onion
- 1 leek
- 1 clove garlic
- 1 bay leaf
- few sprigs parsley
- salt to taste

Place the chicken and beef in a large saucepan with the water. Bring to a boil and skim off any scum that has risen to the top. Add the onion, garlic, leek, bay leaf, and parsley. Season with salt and simmer for about 2 hours. Filter and use as indicated in the recipes.
Makes: 2 quarts/2 liters

Triangular ravioli

Triangle-shaped ravioli are prepared from individual squares of pasta dough. They can be filled with vegetable, meat, or seafood fillings. If liked, large squares of pasta can be cut and filled so that you serve just 3 or 4 ravioli to each guest.

❶

Roll the pasta out into sheets and place on a floured work surface. Use a plain pastry cutter to cut into strips and then into squares.

❷

Place a blob of filling at the center of each square of pasta.

❸

Fold the dough over the blobs of filling to create triangle-shaped filled pasta.

❹

Lightly flour the tines (prongs) of a fork and press down firmly around the edges to seal.

❺

Triangular shaped filled pasta can be made in all sizes, from tiny to large.

Cappelletti

Cappelletti ("little hats"), also known as cappellacci, are also made from small, individually cut squares of fresh pasta. They are then filled and folded into triangles and twisted into their classic shape.

Conserving filled pasta

Making filled pasta requires time and effort so it is a good idea to make a double batch and freeze half for later use. Homemade filled pasta, which will only keep in the refrigerator for up to 2 days, can be kept for several months when frozen. Place the filled pasta in the freezer on a tray in a single layer until solid, then transfer to sealed and labeled plastic bags. Thaw completely before cooking. Filled pasta with potato stuffing is not suitable for freezing.

1

Roll the pasta out into sheets and place on a floured work surface. Use a plain pastry cutter to cut into strips and then into squares.

2

Place a blob of filling at the center of each square of pasta and fold into a triangle shape.

3

Wrap the triangular-shaped piece of pasta around a finger and seal the ends.

4

Slip the finished pasta off your finger and repeat the process with the remaining squares of pasta and filling.

5

Cappelletti have sharp pointed pieces of pasta sticking up at the top, unlike tortellini which are rounded.

Square or rectangular ravioli

Ravioli are generally square or rectangular, with all four sides fluted or three fluted sides and one straight (where the pasta has been folded over). They are usually about 2 inches (5 cm) long. Ravioli can be served in boiling stock, or with vegetable, meat, or seafood fillings.

Cooking filled pasta

All types of homemade fresh pasta have very short cooking times. The length of time will vary, depending on how thick the pasta is and how long it has been rested. As for commercially made dried pasta such as spaghetti, we use the expression "al dente" for when it is ready, although correctly cooked fresh pasta will always be softer and more elastic than the dried variety.

❶

Roll the pasta out into sheets and place on a floured work surface. Cut into strips and place blobs of filling at regular intervals down one half of each strip.

❷

Slightly flatten the blobs of filling. Fold half the pasta sheet over on itself to cover the blobs of filling.

❸

Press down lightly between the blobs of filling with your fingertips to remove excess air.

❹

Use a fluted pastry cutter to cut out the ravioli.

❺

These ravioli will have three fluted edges and one plain edge where they have been folded.

Agnolotti with plin

Agnolotti are a type of ravioli from Piedmont in the northwest. They almost always have a roasted or braised meat filling and are served in boiling stock or with a simple butter and sage sauce. They are usually about 2 inches (5 cm) long. Plin agnolotti are traditionally served at Christmas. The dough is usually a darker yellow than normal fresh pasta because more egg yolks are used.

Serving filled pasta

Filled pasta shapes with meat-based stuffings, such as agnolotti and tortellini, are often served in boiling meat stock. If the pasta has a lighter, vegetable or cheese based stuffing, then it will be very good served in a simple butter and sage sauce. To make the sauce: melt $^1/_2$ cup (125 g) of high-quality, salted butter over low heat. Add 4–6 torn fresh sage leaves and cook for 4–5 minutes, or until the sauce is hazelnut brown. These quantities will make enough sauce for 4–6 people.

❶ Roll the pasta out into sheets and place on a floured work surface. Cut into strips and place small blobs of filling at regular intervals down one side of each strip. Begin folding the pasta over on itself, leaving a strip down the long edge.

❷ Use your fingertips to gently squeeze between each blob of filling as you continue to roll the pasta over on itself.

❸ Use a fluted pastry cutter to trim the extra strip of pasta to about $^1/_2$ inch (1 cm) from the edge.

❹ Fold the pasta over again so that only a thin strip of pasta from the extra strip is showing. Use the fluted pastry cutter to cut between the blobs of filling.

❺ The finished plin agnolotti are quite small and have a distinctive strip of fluted pasta along one edge.

SACCOTTINI ALLE ZUCCHINE
Pasta sacks with zucchini

Pasta
- $3/4$ quantity plain fresh pasta dough (see chart on page 8)
- 2 tablespoons coarse sea salt (to cook the pasta)

Filling
- 14 oz/400 g zucchini/courgettes, cut in small cubes
- scant 1 cup/200 ml extra-virgin olive oil
- 2 tablespoons finely chopped chives
- 1 sprig fresh oregano
- 1 egg, lightly beaten
- 2 tablespoons freshly grated Parmesan cheese
- salt and freshly ground white pepper to taste

Sauce
- 1 lb/500 g zucchini/courgettes
- salt and freshly ground black pepper to taste
- scant 1 cup/200 ml extra-virgin olive oil
- 4 tablespoons chile-flavored extra-virgin olive oil
- 1 tablespoon finely chopped chives

Prepare the pasta dough following the instructions on pages 9–11. Let rest for 30 minutes. • Filling: Heat the oil in a small skillet (frying pan) or deep fryer to very hot. Add the cubes of zucchini in batches and fry until golden brown. Drain on paper towels. • Transfer the fried zucchini to a bowl and mix in the chives, oregano, egg, Parmesan, salt, and pepper. • Divide the pasta dough into 5 pieces. Roll it through the machine one notch at a time down to the second thinnest setting. Cut the dough into disks about 2 inches (5 cm) in diameter. • Place a teaspoon of filling in the center of each disk and pull the pasta up around it as if it were a sack. Squeeze the tops together to close. If the pasta does not stick together, brush it with a little water around the tops just before you seal them. • Place a large pan of water over high heat with the coarse sea salt. Cover and bring to a boil. • Sauce: Use a zester to obtain long thin "spaghetti" from the green parts of the zucchini. • Place in a large flat bowl and sprinkle with salt. Drain any water from the zucchini and let rest for 15 minutes. • Cook the pasta in batches in the boiling water until al dente, about 3–4 minutes. • While the pasta is cooking, carefully pat the zucchini dry with paper towels. • Heat the oil in a small skillet (frying pan) or deep fryer to very hot. • Fry the "spaghetti" in batches and drain on paper towels. • Drain the pasta carefully and place the little sacks upright in a serving dish. Sprinkle with the crisp green zucchini. Drizzle with the chile-flavored oil and sprinkle with the chives. Grind with pepper and serve immediately.

Serves 4–6; Preparation: 1 hour + time to make the pasta; Cooking: 45 minutes; Level 3

FAGOTTINI ALLE MELANZANE
Eggplant ravioli

Pasta
- $1/2$ quantity plain fresh pasta dough (see chart on page 8)
- 2 tablespoons coarse sea salt (to cook the pasta)

Filling
- 1 whole eggplant/aubergine, weighing about 10 oz/300 g
- salt and freshly ground black pepper to taste
- 1 tablespoon finely chopped parsley
- pinch of oregano
- 5 leaves fresh basil, torn
- 1 egg
- 4 tablespoons freshly grated Parmesan cheese
- about 4 tablespoons fine dry bread crumbs

Sauce
- 4 tablespoons extra-virgin olive oil
- 1 clove garlic, crushed with the back of a knife but whole
- $1^1/2$ lb/1.25 kg ripe tomatoes, peeled, seeds gently squeezed out, cut in $1/2$-inch/1-cm cubes
- salt and freshly ground black pepper to taste
- 5 oz/150 g Mozzarella cheese (preferably top quality Neapolitan water buffalo), cut in small cubes

Prepare the pasta dough following the instructions on pages 9–11. Let rest for 30 minutes. • Filling: Preheat the oven to 400°F/200°C/gas 6. • Bake the eggplant in the oven for about 30 minutes, or until slightly dark in color and tender when pressed with a fingertip. • Cut the eggplant in half and use a tablespoon to scoop out the flesh. Place in a bowl and break up with a fork. Season with salt and let rest for 30 minutes. • Place the eggplant in a clean cloth and squeeze gently to remove excess water. • Return to a bowl and mash with a fork. Season with pepper, parsley, oregano, and basil. Add the egg, Parmesan, and enough bread crumbs to make a firm dough (about the same as meatballs). Refrigerate until ready to use. • Divide the pasta dough into 2 pieces. Roll it through the machine one notch at a time down to the second thinnest setting. Cut into 4 x 6-inch (10 x 15-cm) rectangles. • Place 2 tablespoons of filling on half of each rectangle and fold the other half over the top. Use a fork to seal the 3 edges of the pasta. Place on a floured cloth until ready to cook. • Place a large pan of water over high heat with the coarse sea salt. Cover and bring to a boil. • Sauce: Heat the oil in a large skillet (frying pan) and sauté the garlic until it turns pale gold. • Discard the garlic. Add the tomatoes and cook over high heat for 3 minutes. Season with salt, pepper, and oregano. • Cook the pasta in the boiling water until al dente, about 4 minutes. • Drain carefully and place in a heated serving dish. Sprinkle with the Mozzarella and spoon the tomato sauce over the top. • Serve immediately.

Serves 4; Preparation: 1 hour 30 minutes + time to make the pasta; Cooking: 45 minutes; Level 3

AGNOLOTTI
Piedmontese ravioli

Pasta
- 3^1/$_3$ cups/500 g all-purpose/plain flour
- 2 eggs
- 5 egg yolks
- few tablespoons cold water

Filling
- 7 oz/200 g roast meat (pork, beef, or chicken), fat removed
- 3^1/$_2$ oz/100 g spinach, boiled and well-rinsed
- 4 tablespoons freshly grated Parmesan cheese
- 2 eggs
- 4–6 tablespoons fine dry bread crumbs
- salt and freshly ground black pepper to taste
- pinch of freshly grated nutmeg

Prepare the pasta dough using the flour, eggs, egg yolks, and water following the instructions on pages 9–11 to obtain a firm dough. Let rest for 20 minutes. • Filling: Process the roast meat and spinach in a food processor until very finely chopped. • Transfer to a bowl and add the Parmesan, eggs, and enough bread crumbs to obtain a soft filling. Season with salt, pepper, and nutmeg and mix well. • Divide the dough into 5–6 pieces. Roll it through the machine one notch at a time down to the second thinnest setting. Cut into long strips about 3 inches (8 cm) wide. • Place heaped teaspoons of filling almost down the center of each strip. Fold the pasta over the filling, slightly crushing the heaps of filling, and pressing your fingers between them. • Use a fluted pastry cutter to cut out the agnolotti (which will have three fluted sides and one smooth one). Place the agnolotti on a clean cloth lightly sprinkled with flour. • Place a large pan of water over high heat with the coarse sea salt. Cover and bring to a boil. • Cook the pasta in the boiling water until al dente, about 3–4 minutes. • Drain well and serve immediately in boiling stock or with a meat or tomato sauce (Try them, for example, with the meat sauce in the recipe for *Potato and pumpkin tortelli* on page 106.)

Serves 4–6: Preparation: 1 hour + time to make the pasta; Cooking: 20 minutes; Level 3

ANOLINI
Anolini in beef stock

Filling
- 14 oz/400 g lean beef, in a single piece
- 2 oz/30 g lard, in a ^{1}/$_2$ x 2^1/$_2$-inch (1 x 6-cm) strip
- salt and freshly ground black pepper to taste
- pinch of freshly grated nutmeg
- 4 tablespoons butter, cut up
- 2 oz/60 g finely chopped onion
- 1^1/$_4$ quarts/1.25 liters Meat stock (see page 97)
- ^{1}/$_2$ cup/75 g fine dry bread crumbs
- ^{1}/$_2$ cup/60 g freshly grated Parmesan cheese
- 1 egg

Pasta
- 1^1/$_3$ cups/200 g all-purpose/plain flour
- 2 eggs
- 1 tablespoon water

Filling: Place the lard on the piece of beef and tie with kitchen string. Season with salt, pepper, and nutmeg. • Melt the butter in a large saucepan and sauté the meat over high heat until browned all over. • Add the onion and sauté for 4 minutes. • Pour in a scant cup (200 ml) of stock. Cover and cook over low heat for 3 hours, or until the meat is falling apart. • Remove from the heat and let cool. • Chop the meat with its cooking juices in a food processor. • Transfer to a bowl and add the bread crumbs, Parmesan, and egg. Season with salt and pepper and refrigerate until ready to use. • While the beef is cooking, prepare the pasta dough using the flour, egg, and water and following the instructions on pages 9–11. Let rest for 30 minutes. • Divide the dough into 4 pieces. Roll it through the machine one notch at a time down to the thinnest setting. Use a fluted round pastry or cookie cutter to cut into 1-inch (2.5-cm) disks. • Place small blobs of filling in the center of half of the disks and cover with other disks of pasta, pressing down around the edges to seal. Place on a floured cloth until ready to cook. • Place the stock over high heat. Cover and bring to a boil. • Cook the pasta in batches in the boiling stock until al dente, about 3 minutes. • Ladle the pasta and stock into individual bowls. • Serve immediately.

Serves 4: Preparation: 1 hour 30 minutes + time to make the pasta; Cooking: 3 hours 30 minutes; Level 3

CONSOMMÉ CON RAVIOLINI
Consommé with small ravioli

Lambrusco is a sparkling medium or dry red wine from the Emilia-Romagna region of central Italy. It is widely available outside Italy but if you can't find it, replace with the same quantity of any other sparkling medium or dry red.

Pasta
- $1/2$ quantity plain fresh pasta dough (see chart on page 8)
- 2 tablespoons coarse sea salt (to cook the pasta)

Filling
- $3^1/2$ oz/100 g speck or smoked bacon, finely chopped
- 1 egg yolk
- 2 tablespoons freshly grated Parmesan cheese
- salt and freshly ground white pepper to taste
- 5 oz/150 g fresh Ricotta cheese, drained

Consommé
- 2 oz/60 g ground/minced beef
- $1/2$ carrot, finely chopped
- $1/2$ leek, finely chopped
- $1/2$ stalk celery, finely chopped
- 1 egg white
- 1 quart/1 liter Meat stock (see page 97), fat skimmed off the top
- 2 cups/500 ml Lambrusco wine

Prepare the pasta dough following the instructions on pages 9–11. Let rest for 30 minutes. • Filling: Mix the speck, egg yolk, Parmesan, and Ricotta. Season with salt and pepper. Refrigerate until ready to use. • Divide the pasta dough into 4 pieces. Roll it through the machine one notch at a time down to the second thinnest setting. • Cut into 1-inch (2.5-cm) strips. • Place marble-sized blobs of filling down the center of half of the strips, spacing them about 1 inch (2.5 cm) apart. Cover with the remaining strips and press down on the edges to seal. Use a fluted pastry cutter to cut into small ravioli about 1-inch (2.5-cm) square. Place on a floured cloth until ready to cook. • Consommé: Place the beef, carrot, leek, celery, and egg white in a medium saucepan and add half the stock. Bring to a boil, stirring gently until the liquid begins to evaporate. Stop stirring and wait for the egg white to come to the surface, filtering all impurities. Boil for a few minutes, then strain through a cloth without breaking the egg white. • Return to the heat and bring to a boil. Remove from the heat and add the wine. • Place the remaining stock over high heat. Cover and bring to a boil. • Cook the pasta in batches in the boiling stock until al dente, about 3 minutes. • Drain well and place in the clarified stock. • Serve immediately.

Serves 4; Preparation: 1 hour + time to make the pasta; Cooking: 30 minutes; Level 3

AGNOLOTTI AL PLIN CON FONDUTA
Christmas agnolotti

Pasta
- 2 cups/300 g all-purpose flour
- 1 very fresh large egg
- 3 very fresh large egg yolks
- few tablespoons cold water

Filling
- 10 oz/300 g roasted meat (pork, beef, or chicken), fat removed
- 4 oz/125 g mortadella
- 1 cup/125 g freshly grated Parmesan cheese
- 1 egg
- scant $1/2$ cup/100 ml fresh cream
- 2 handfuls fresh bread crumbs, soaked in milk and squeezed dry
- salt and freshly ground black pepper to taste
- pinch of freshly grated nutmeg

Sauce
- 5 oz/150 g Fontina cheese, cut into cubes and soaked in $3^1/2$ tablespoons milk in the refrigerator for 2 hours
- 3 egg yolks
- 2 tablespoons butter, cut up
- salt and freshly ground white pepper to taste

Prepare the pasta dough using the flour, eggs, egg yolks, and water following the instructions on pages 9–11. Let rest for 20 minutes. • Filling: Process the roast meat and mortadella in a food processor until very finely chopped. • Transfer to a bowl and add the Parmesan, egg, cream, and bread crumbs. Season with salt, pepper, and nutmeg and mix well. • Divide the pasta dough into 5–6 pieces. Roll it through the machine one notch at a time down to the second thinnest setting. Cut into long strips about $2^1/2$ inches (6 cm) wide. • Place heaping teaspoons of filling almost down the center of each strip. Proceed as shown on page 101. Place the agnolotti on a clean cloth lightly sprinkled with flour. • Sauce: Place the cheese and milk, egg yolks, and butter in a double boiler over barely simmering water. Stir with a wooden spoon until the cheese has melted. Beat with a wire whisk until the eggs thicken and the sauce is thick and creamy. Do not overcook as the eggs can easily curdle. Remove from the heat and season with salt and pepper. Keep warm, stirring often until ready to use. • Place a large pan of water over high heat with the coarse sea salt. Cover and bring to a boil. • Cook the pasta in batches in the boiling water until al dente, about 3–4 minutes. • Drain well and serve immediately with the cheese sauce poured over the top.

Serves 4–6; Preparation: 1 hour 30 minutes + time to make the pasta; Cooking: 20 minutes; Level 3

Above: Consommé with small ravioli

Below: Christmas agnolotti

RAVIOLO APERTO AI PEPERONI
Open ravioli with bell peppers

Pasta
- 1/2 quantity plain fresh pasta dough (see chart on page 8)
- 2 tablespoons coarse sea salt (to cook the pasta)
- 2 tablespoons extra-virgin olive oil (to cook the pasta)

Filling
- 4 tablespoons extra-virgin olive oil
- 1 white onion, finely chopped
- 1/2 carrot, finely chopped
- 1/2 stalk celery, finely chopped
- salt and freshly ground black pepper to taste
- 3 1/2 oz/100 g pancetta, cut in cubes
- 1 lb/500 g yellow bell peppers/capsicums, cut in julienne strips (matchsticks)
- 2 tablespoons butter, cut up
- 1 cup/125 g freshly grated Parmesan cheese
- 1 tablespoon finely chopped parsley

Prepare the pasta following the instructions on pages 9–11. Let rest for 30 minutes. • Place a large pan of water over high heat with half the coarse sea salt and oil. Cover and bring to a boil. • Divide the pasta into 4 pieces. Roll each piece through the machine one notch at a time down to the thinnest setting. Cut into sheets about 5 inches (13 cm) square. • Cook the sheets of pasta following the instructions for lasagne on page 66. Place on a damp cloth until ready to serve. • Filling: Heat the oil in a large skillet (frying pan) and cook the onion, carrot, and celery with a pinch of salt over low heat for 15 minutes. • Add the pancetta and cook for 5 minutes. • Increase the heat to medium and add the bell peppers. Season with salt and pepper. Cover and cook for 20 minutes, or until tender. • Stir in the butter. • Spoon a layer of filling into 4 heated individual serving plates and cover with a piece of pasta. Spoon the remaining sauce over the pasta and sprinkle with half the Parmesan. Top with a layer of pasta, placed to form a star-shape in each dish. Sprinkle with the remaining Parmesan, garnish with the parsley, and serve immediately.

Serves 4; Preparation: 30 minutes + time to make the pasta; Cooking: 50 minutes; Level 2

TORTELLI DI ZUCCA E PATATE
Potato and pumpkin tortelli

Pasta
- 3/4 quantity plain fresh pasta dough (see chart on page 8)
- 2 tablespoons coarse sea salt (to cook the pasta)

Sauce
- 4 tablespoons extra-virgin olive oil
- 1 red onion, finely chopped
- 1 carrot, finely chopped
- 1 stalk celery, finely chopped
- salt and freshly ground black pepper to taste
- 1 clove garlic, finely chopped
- 1/2 oz/15 g dried porcini mushrooms, soaked in cold water for 2 hours, drained, and finely chopped
- 8 oz/250 g ground/minced beef
- 1 tablespoon all-purpose/plain flour
- 1/2 cup/125 ml dry red wine (passata)
- 1 lb/500 g canned tomatoes, strained
- 1 tablespoon finely chopped parsley
- pinch of freshly grated nutmeg

Filling
- 10 oz/300 g winter squash or pumpkin, cut in pieces but not peeled
- 1 lb/500 g potatoes
- 1 1/2 tablespoons butter
- 2 tablespoons freshly grated Parmesan cheese
- pinch of freshly grated nutmeg
- salt and freshly ground black pepper to taste

To serve
- 3/4 cup/90 g freshly grated Parmesan cheese
- freshly ground black pepper to taste

Prepare the pasta dough following the instructions on pages 9–11. Let rest for 30 minutes. • Sauce: Heat the oil in a medium saucepan and sauté the onion, carrot, celery with a pinch of salt over low heat for 15 minutes. • Add the garlic and mushrooms and cook for 2 minutes. • Add the beef and sauté over high heat until well browned. • Stir in the flour and cook for 2 minutes. • Pour in the wine and cook until evaporated. • Stir in the tomatoes, parsley, and nutmeg. Season with salt and pepper. Cover and cook over low heat for at least 1 hour, stirring occasionally. • Filling: Preheat the oven to 400°F/200°C/ gas 6. • Bake the pumpkin until tender, about 1 hour. Remove and let cool. • Use a tablespoon to scoop out the flesh. Transfer to a food processor and process until pureed. • Boil the potatoes in lightly salted water in their jackets until tender. • Drain and slip off the skins. Mash in a large bowl with the butter, Parmesan, nutmeg, salt, and pepper until smooth. • Mix in the pumpkin puree until well blended. • Divide the pasta dough into 4–5 pieces. Roll it through the machine one notch at a time down to the second thinnest setting. Cut into 4-inch (10-cm) wide strips. • Place walnut-sized blobs of filling down the center of each strip, about 3/4 inch (2 cm) apart. Fold the pasta over the filling and press down lightly with your fingertips to seal. Use a fluted pastry cutter to cut out the tortelli. Place on a floured cloth until ready to cook. • Place a large pan of water over high heat with the coarse sea salt. Cover and bring to a boil. • Cook the pasta in batches in the boiling water until al dente, about 3 minutes. • Drain and arrange in layers in a heated serving dish, alternating the pasta, meat sauce, and Parmesan. Grind generously with pepper and serve immediately.

Serves 4–6: Preparation: 1 hour + time to make the pasta; Cooking: 1 hour 45 minutes; Level 3

Potato and pumpkin tortelli

RAVIOLI CON FUNGHI
Ravioli with mushrooms

Pasta
- 1 1/3 cups/200 g all-purpose flour
- 1 very fresh large egg
- about 4 tablespoons cold water

Filling
- 1 oz/30 g dried porcini mushrooms, soaked in water for 1 hour at room temperature
- 2 tablespoons extra-virgin olive oil
- 1 clove garlic, finely chopped
- 1 sprig fresh rosemary
- 1 bay leaf
- 7 oz/200 g ground/minced pork
- 1 shallot, finely chopped
- 2 tablespoons brandy
- 1 tablespoon finely chopped parsley
- 1 egg
- 4 tablespoons freshly grated Parmesan cheese
- salt and freshly ground black pepper to taste

To serve
- 6–8 tablespoons freshly grated Parmesan cheese
- 3 sprigs fresh marjoram, finely chopped
- 6 tablespoons melted butter

Prepare the pasta dough using the flour, egg, and water following the instructions on pages 9–11. Let rest for 30 minutes. • Filling: Drain the mushrooms, reserving the liquid. Chop the mushrooms finely. • Heat the oil in a large skillet (frying pan) and sauté the garlic, rosemary, and bay leaf over high heat for 1 minute. • Add the pork, shallot, and mushrooms. Add the brandy and cook until evaporated. • Cook over medium heat for 10 minutes, stirring often, and adding a little of the mushroom liquid if the sauce dries out. • Discard the bay leaf and rosemary. Transfer the mixture to a food processor and chop finely. • Transfer to a bowl and add the parsley, egg, and Parmesan. Season with salt and pepper. • Place a large pan of water over high heat with the coarse sea salt. Cover and bring to a boil. • Divide the dough into 3 pieces. Roll it through the machine one notch at a time down to the thinnest setting. Cut the dough into circles about 2 1/2 inches (6 cm) in diameter. • Form tablespoons of filling into balls about the size of walnuts. Place one at the center of half of the pieces of pasta. Cover each one with another piece of pasta to form round ravioli. • Cook the pasta in the boiling water until al dente, about 2–3 minutes. Drain well and transfer to a serving dish. • Sprinkle with the Parmesan and marjoram and drizzle with the butter. • Serve immediately.

Serves 4; Preparation: 1 hour + time to make the pasta; Cooking: 1 hour; Level 3

SOMBRERI CON UOVO
Mexican hats with egg

Pasta
- 1/2 quantity plain fresh pasta dough (see chart on page 8)
- 2 tablespoons coarse sea salt (to cook the pasta)

Filling
- 7 oz/200 g fresh Ricotta cheese, drained
- 1 egg
- 4 tablespoons freshly grated Parmesan cheese
- 1 tablespoon finely chopped parsley
- salt and freshly ground white pepper to taste
- 4 egg yolks

Sauce
- 10 oz/300 g asparagus, stalks trimmed and peeled
- 3 tablespoons butter
- 4 tablespoons freshly grated Pecorino cheese
- freshly ground black pepper to taste

Prepare the pasta dough following the instructions on pages 9–11. Let rest for 30 minutes. • Filling: Stir the Ricotta in a medium bowl until smooth and creamy. Add the whole egg, Parmesan, and parsley. Season with salt and pepper. • Transfer to a pastry bag fitted with a 1-inch (2.5-cm) tip and refrigerate until ready to use. • Place a large pan of water over high heat with the coarse sea salt. Cover and bring to a boil. • Sauce: Separate the asparagus stalks from the tips. Cook the stalks in the boiling water for 3 minutes, then add the tips. Remove the asparagus with a slotted spoon and set aside. Return the water to the heat. • Melt the butter in a medium skillet (frying pan) and sauté the asparagus for 3 minutes. Remove from the heat and keep warm. • Divide the pasta dough into 4 pieces. Roll each piece through the machine one notch at a time down to the thinnest setting. Cut each piece into two disks, one measuring 6 inches (15 cm) in diameter and the other 5 inches (13 cm) in diameter. • Pipe a ring of ravioli filling around the edge of the smaller disk, leaving a 1-inch (2.5-cm) border. Use a tablespoon to place an egg yolk in the center of each ring of filling. Cover each disk with the larger piece of pasta, pressing down on the edges to seal. • Place each "sombrero" on a piece of waxed paper. The prepared pasta should be left as short a time as possible before cooking. If left for a long time the Ricotta will dampen the pasta, causing it to break during cooking. • Slip the pasta into the boiling water (used to cook the asparagus) using the waxed paper very carefully to prevent them from breaking. Cook each one separately for 1 minute. • Spoon the asparagus sauce into 4 individual serving plates and place one sombrero in each. Sprinkle with the Pecorino and a generous grinding of pepper. • Serve immediately.

Serves 4; Preparation: 1 hour + time to make the pasta; Cooking: 40 minutes; Level 3

Above: Ravioli with mushrooms

Below: Mexican hats with egg

RAVIOLI DI BROCCOLI ALLA SALSA DI ACCIUGHE
Broccoli ravioli with anchovy sauce

Pasta
- $1/2$ quantity plain fresh pasta dough (see chart on page 8)
- 2 tablespoons coarse sea salt (to cook the pasta)

Filling
- $2^1/2$ lb/1.25 kg broccoli
- 10 oz/300 g boiled floury potatoes, mashed
- 2 cloves garlic, finely chopped
- 2 tablespoons extra-virgin olive oil
- 1 tablespoon finely chopped parsley
- $1/2$ teaspoon red pepper flakes
- salt to taste

Sauce
- 4 tablespoons extra-virgin olive oil
- $1/2$ onion, finely chopped
- salt to taste
- 8 anchovy fillets, finely chopped
- 3 cloves garlic, finely chopped
- 4 tablespoons dry white wine
- 4 tablespoons toasted dry bread crumbs
- 4 tablespoons freshly grated aged Pecorino cheese

Prepare the pasta dough following the instructions on pages 9–11. Let rest for 30 minutes. • Filling: Peel the broccoli stalks and chop into small dice. Divide the heads into florets. Place the stalks in a steamer and sprinkle with salt. Cook for 10 minutes. • Add the florets and cook for 10 more minutes, or until tender. • Transfer to a food processor and chop until smooth. • Place the mixture in a large skillet (frying pan) and cook, stirring often, over medium-low heat for 4 minutes to remove any extra moisture. • Mix the mashed potatoes, chopped broccoli, garlic, oil, parsley, red pepper flakes, and salt. • Transfer the mixture to a pastry bag and refrigerate until ready to use. • Sauce: Heat the oil in a medium skillet (frying pan). Cover and cook the onion and a pinch of salt over low heat for 10 minutes. • Add the anchovies and garlic and stir constantly until the anchovies have dissolved. • Pour in the wine and cook until evaporated. • Divide the dough into 3–4 pieces. Roll it through the machine one notch at a time down to the thinnest setting. Cut the dough into long strips about $2^1/2$ inches (6 cm) wide. • Pipe blobs of filling about the size of a walnut on half the strips of pasta leaving spaces of about 1 inch (2.5 cm) between each one. Cover the strips of pasta with the remaining strips, pressing down between the filling and along the edges to seal. Use a fluted pastry cutter to cut out the ravioli. Carefully transfer the ravioli onto a lightly floured cloth until ready to cook. • Place a large pan of water over high heat with the coarse sea salt. Cover and bring to a boil. • Cook the pasta in batches in the boiling water until al dente, about 2–3 minutes. • Drain well and transfer to a serving dish. • Pour the anchovy sauce over the top and sprinkle with the toasted bread crumbs and Pecorino. • Serve immediately.

Serves 4; Preparation: 45 minutes + time to make the pasta; Cooking: 45 minutes; Level 3

RAVIOLINI DI PECORINO IN SALSA DI FAVE
Pecorino ravioli with fava bean sauce

Sauce
- 6 tablespoons butter, cut up
- 1 leek, cut in thin wheels
- 10 oz/300 g fresh hulled fava/broad beans
- salt and freshly ground black pepper to taste
- about $1^1/4$ cups/310 ml Meat stock (see page 97)

Pasta
- $3/4$ quantity plain fresh pasta dough (see chart on page 8)
- 2 tablespoons coarse sea salt (to cook the pasta)

Filling
- 5 oz/150 g fresh Ricotta cheese, drained
- $1^3/4$ cups/215 g coarsely grated young Pecorino cheese
- salt and freshly ground white pepper to taste
- pinch of freshly grated nutmeg

Sauce: Melt the butter in a small saucepan and sauté the leek over low heat for 10 minutes. • Add the fava beans. Season with salt and pour in the stock. Cover and cook over low heat for about 1 hour, stirring often, adding more stock if the beans begin to dry. • Season with salt and pepper and chop in a food processor until smooth. • Prepare the pasta dough following the instructions on pages 9–11. Let rest for 30 minutes. • Filling: Strain the Ricotta into a medium bowl. Add the Pecorino and season with salt, pepper, and nutmeg. Refrigerate until ready to use. • Divide the dough into 4 pieces. Roll it through the machine one notch at a time down to the second thinnest setting. Cut into 2-inch (5-cm) wide strips. • Place tablespoons of filling down the center of half the strips, leaving about 1 inch (2.5 cm) between each blob of filling. Cover with other strips, pressing down between the blobs of filling and along the edges to seal. Use a fluted round pastry or cookie cutter to cut into $1^1/2$-inch (3–4-cm) disks. • Place on a floured cloth until ready to cook. • Place a large pan of water over high heat with the coarse sea salt. Cover and bring to a boil. • Reheat the fava bean sauce. • Cook the pasta in batches in the boiling water until al dente, about 2–3 minutes. • Spread a layer of fava bean sauce over a serving plate. Drain the pasta and place on top of the sauce. Spoon the remaining sauce over the top and season with pepper. • Serve immediately.

Serves 4; Preparation: 45 minutes + time to make the pasta; Cooking: 1 hour 30 minutes; Level 2

Pecorino ravioli with fava bean sauce

RAVIOLI AI CARCIOFI
Artichoke ravioli

Pasta
- • ¹/₂ quantity plain fresh pasta dough (see chart on page 8)
- • 2 tablespoons coarse sea salt (to cook the pasta)

Filling
- • 4 artichokes
- • juice of 1 lemon
- • 2 tablespoons butter
- • 1 scallion, finely chopped
- • salt and freshly ground white pepper to taste
- • 8 walnuts, shelled and coarsely chopped
- • 4 tablespoons milk
- • ³/₄ cup/90 g freshly grated Parmesan cheese
- • 1 egg
- • ¹/₂ cup/75 g fine dry bread crumbs

Sauce
- • 5 tablespoons melted butter
- • 4 tablespoons freshly grated Parmesan cheese

Prepare the pasta dough following the instructions on pages 9–11. Let rest for 30 minutes. • Filling: Clean the artichokes by removing the tough outer leaves. Chop off the top third of the leaves and cut in half. Remove any fuzzy choke. Chop them coarsely and place in a bowl of cold water with the lemon juice. • Melt the butter in a medium saucepan and sweat the scallion with a pinch of salt over low heat for 10 minutes. • Drain the artichokes and add to the saucepan along with the walnuts. Season with salt and pepper. Cover and cook over low heat for 40 minutes, gradually adding the milk. Let cool. • Chop the filling in a food processor. Transfer to a bowl and add the Parmesan, egg, and enough of the bread crumbs to obtain a firm mixture. • Divide the pasta dough into 4 pieces. Roll it through the machine one notch at a time down to the second thinnest setting. Cut the dough into long strips about 3 inches (8 cm) wide. • Place ¹/₂ tablespoons of filling shaped into balls down the strips of pasta leaving about 1 inch (2.5 cm) between them. Fold the strips of pasta over to cover the blobs of filling, pressing down between each blob and along the edges to seal. Use a fluted pastry cutter to cut into ravioli measuring about 1 x 2 inches (5 x 3 cm). Carefully transfer the ravioli onto a lightly floured cloth until ready to cook. • Place a large pan of water over high heat with the coarse sea salt. Cover and bring to a boil. • Cook the pasta in batches in the boiling water until al dente, about 2–3 minutes. Drain well and transfer to a serving dish. • Drizzle with the butter and sprinkle with the Parmesan. • Serve immediately.

Serves 4; Preparation: 1 hour 30 minutes + time to make the pasta; Cooking: 1 hour; Level 3

RAVIOLI AL LATTE CON PESCE
Milk ravioli with beans and tuna

This recipe calls for a scant cup (about 200 ml) of cannellini bean purée. This can be made by soaking 3¹/₂ oz (100 g) of dried cannellini beans in cold water overnight. Cook them with 1 tablespoon of extra-virgin olive oil, 1 fresh sage leaf, and 1 clove of garlic for about 90 minutes. When the beans are tender, drain well and chop in a food processor until pureed.

Pasta
- • 1¹/₃ cups/200 g durum or hard wheat flour
- • ¹/₃ cup/90 ml milk
- • few tablespoons cold water
- • 2 tablespoons coarse sea salt (to cook the pasta)

Filling
- • 8 oz/250 g mashed potatoes
- • scant 1 cup/200 ml cannellini bean purée (see above)
- • 1 tablespoon extra-virgin olive oil
- • salt and freshly ground black pepper to taste

Sauce
- • 2 tablespoons chile-flavored extra-virgin olive oil
- • 1 clove garlic, crushed
- • 7 oz/200 g tuna preserved in olive oil, drained
- • 1 scallion/spring onion, finely chopped

Prepare the pasta dough using the flour, milk, and water, following the instructions on pages 9–11. Let rest for 30 minutes. • Filling: Mix the mashed potatoes, bean purée, oil, salt, and pepper in a medium bowl. • Divide the dough into 5 pieces. Roll it through the machine one notch at a time down to the second thinnest setting. Cut the dough into pieces about 2¹/₂ inches (6 cm) square. • Place a teaspoon of filling in the center of each piece of pasta. Fold the pasta over the filling to form triangles, pressing the edges down well to seal. • Place the ravioli on a clean dry cloth and sprinkle with hard wheat flour. • Place a large pan of water over high heat with the coarse sea salt. Cover and bring to a boil. • Sauce: Heat the chile-flavored oil and garlic in a small saucepan. • Add the tuna, breaking it up with a fork. Cook for 3–4 minutes, or until heated through. • Cook the pasta in batches in the boiling water until al dente, about 3–4 minutes. • Drain the pasta well and transfer to a serving dish. Drizzle with the sauce, sprinkle with the scallion, and serve immediately.

Serves 4; Preparation: 45 minutes + time to make the pasta + time to soak the beans; Cooking: 15 minutes + time to cook the beans; Level 3

Milk ravioli with beans and tuna

RAVIOLI THAI STYLE
Ravioli Thai-style

Filling
• 7 oz/200 g cabbage, thinly sliced
• salt to taste
• 7 oz/200 g ground/minced pork
• 2 tablespoons finely chopped lemon grass
• 1 small carrot, finely chopped
• 3 scallions/spring onions, finely chopped
• 1 tablespoon soy sauce
• 2 tablespoons sherry
• 1 tablespoon cornstarch/cornflour
• 1 teaspoon finely chopped fresh ginger root
• pinch of sugar
Pasta
• 1 cup/150 g all-purpose/plain flour
• $1/3$ cup/50 g hard wheat flour
• 1 tablespoon peanut oil
• scant 1 cup/100 ml warm water

Place the cabbage in a large bowl and rub in 2–3 pinches of salt. Set aside for 1 hour. • Prepare the pasta dough using the two flours, oil, and enough water to obtain a firm dough following the instructions on pages 9–11. Let rest for 30 minutes. • Squeeze the cabbage to remove excess water. Return to the bowl and add the pork, lemon grass, carrot, scallions, soy sauce, sherry, cornstarch, ginger root, and sugar. Use your hands to mix it well. Refrigerate until ready to use. • Divide the dough into 4 pieces. Roll it through the machine one notch at a time down to the thinnest setting. Cut the dough into disks about 3 inches (8 cm) in diameter. • Place a heaping tablespoon of filling in the center of each disk of pasta. Pull the pasta over the top to form half-moon shapes and pinch the edges to seal. If the pasta is too dry to seal, brush the edges with a little warm water. • Place a large pan of water over high heat. Cover and bring to a boil. • Place the ravioli well spaced in an oriental steamer over the boiling water and cook for 10 minutes. • Serve hot with soy sauce.

Serves 4; Preparation: 45 minutes + time to rest the cabbage and make the pasta; Cooking: 10 minutes; Level 3

CAPPELLETTI DIVERSI
Cappelletti with Jerusalem artichokes

Pasta
• $3/4$ quantity plain fresh pasta dough (see chart on page 8)
• 2 tablespoons coarse sea salt (to cook the pasta)
Filling
• 2 tablespoons butter, cut up
• 3 oz/90 g turkey breast, chopped
• 4 oz/125 g chicken breast, chopped
• 2 oz/60 g pancetta, chopped
• 2 oz/60 g lean veal or beef, chopped
• 4 tablespoons ground almonds
• 1 egg
• 2 oz/60 g creamy fresh goat's cheese
• 2 tablespoons freshly grated Parmesan cheese
• salt and freshly ground black pepper to taste
• pinch of freshly grated nutmeg
Sauce
• 2 tablespoons butter
• 10 oz/300 g Jerusalem artichokes, peeled and cut into small cubes
• scant 1 cup/200 ml Meat stock (see page 97)
• scant 1 cup/200 ml heavy/double cream
• salt and freshly ground black pepper to taste
• $1/2$ cup/60 g freshly grated Parmesan cheese

Prepare the pasta dough following the instructions on pages 9–11. Let rest for 30 minutes. • Filling: Melt the butter in a small saucepan and sauté the turkey, chicken, pancetta, and veal over medium heat for 5 minutes, or until the meat is lightly browned. • Remove from the heat and chop the meat and cooking juices in a food processor. • Transfer to a bowl and add the almonds, egg, goat's cheese, and Parmesan. Season with salt, pepper, and nutmeg. • Divide the dough into 4 pieces. Roll it through the machine one notch at a time down to the thinnest setting. Cut the dough into 2-inch (5-cm) squares. • Form scant teaspoons of filling into small balls. Place one at the center of each piece of pasta and shape into cappelletti following the instructions on page 99. • Place a large pan of water over high heat with the coarse sea salt. Cover and bring to a boil. • Sauce: Melt the butter in a medium saucepan and sauté the Jerusalem artichokes for 3 minutes. • Pour in the stock and simmer over medium heat for 15 minutes. If it dries out during cooking, add a little more stock or water. • Remove from the heat and chop in a food processor with the cream. Season with salt and pepper. • Transfer the sauce to a skillet. • Cook the pasta in batches in the boiling water until al dente, about 3–4 minutes. • Drain well and add to the skillet with the sauce. Cook for 2–3 minutes, stirring carefully. Sprinkle with the Parmesan and a generous grinding of pepper and serve.

Serves 4–6; Preparation: 45 minutes + time to make the pasta; Cooking: 40 minutes; Level 3

Cappelletti with Jerusalem artichokes

CAPPELLACCI MELANZANE E CIOCCOLATO
Cappellacci with eggplant and chocolate

Pasta
- $3/4$ quantity plain fresh pasta dough (see chart on page 8)
- 2 tablespoons coarse sea salt (to cook the pasta)

Sauce
- 1 tablespoon extra-virgin olive oil
- 1 lb/500 g ripe tomatoes, peeled, seeded, and cut in small cubes
- $1/2$ small red onion, finely chopped
- 1 clove garlic, finely chopped
- 4–5 leaves fresh basil, torn
- pinch of sugar
- salt to taste
- 4 tablespoons melted butter

Filling
- 1 medium eggplant/aubergine
- 1 tablespoon extra-virgin olive oil
- 1 tablespoon finely chopped white onion
- 1 ripe tomato, peeled, seeded, and cut in small cubes
- $1/4$ teaspoon red pepper flakes
- about 3 tablespoons fine dry bread crumbs
- 1 tablespoon unsweetened cocoa powder
- 5 oz/150 g Ricotta cheese, drained
- 1 oz/30 g high quality chocolate (at least 70% cocoa solids), in flakes
- salt to taste

Prepare the pasta dough following the instructions on pages 9–11. Let rest for 30 minutes. • Sauce: Heat the oil in a medium saucepan and add the tomatoes, onion, garlic, basil, and sugar. Season with salt. Cover and cook over low heat for 40 minutes. If the sauce is too liquid, uncover and cook until it reduces a little. • Transfer to a food processor and process until smooth. • Filling: Preheat the oven to 350°F/180°C/ gas 4. • Cut the eggplant in half lengthwise without peeling it. Use a sharp knife to make deep cuts crosswise in the flesh, without piercing the skin. • Bake for about 1 hour, or until tender. • Let the eggplant cool, then use a tablespoon to scoop out the flesh. • Heat the oil in a medium skillet (frying pan) and sauté the onion over low heat for 10 minutes. • Add the tomato, eggplant, and red pepper flakes. Cook over high heat for 10 minutes. Season with salt and remove from the heat. • Let cool, then stir in the bread crumbs and cocoa. • Chop in a food processor, then stir in one-third of the Ricotta. • Divide the pasta dough into 4 pieces. Roll it through the machine one notch at a time down to the thinnest setting. Cut into 3-inch (8-cm) squares. • Place 1 tablespoon of filling, $1/2$ tablespoon of Ricotta, and a flake of chocolate in the center of each square of pasta. Fold over into triangular shapes and shape into cappellacci following the instructions on page 99. • Place a large pan of water over high heat with the coarse sea salt. Cover and bring to a boil. • Cook the pasta in batches in the boiling water until al dente, about 2–3 minutes. • Spoon the hot tomato sauce into 4 individual serving plates. • Drain the pasta and place on top of the tomato sauce. • Drizzle with the butter and serve immediately.

Serves 4; Preparation: 1 hour 30 minutes + time to make the pasta; Cooking: 2 hours; Level 3

CAPPELLACCI IN BRODO DI GALLINA
Cappellacci in chicken stock

Stock
- 1 medium boiling chicken, cleaned
- 1 lb/500 g boiling beef
- 4 quarts/4 liters cold water
- 1 yellow onion, peeled
- 1 stalk leek
- 1 clove garlic
- 1 bay leaf
- few sprigs parsley
- salt to taste

Pasta
- $3/4$ quantity plain fresh pasta dough (see chart on page 8
- 2 tablespoons coarse sea salt (to cook the pasta)

Filling
- 2 tablespoons butter, cut up
- $3^{1}/2$ oz/100 g pork, cut in small chunks
- $3^{1}/2$ oz/100 g plain (not spicy), fresh Italian sausage meat
- $3^{1}/2$ oz/100 g turkey breast
- 2 oz/60 g prosciutto/Parma ham
- 2 oz/60 g lean ground/minced veal or beef
- 1 egg
- $1/2$ cup/60 g freshly grated Parmesan cheese
- salt and freshly ground black pepper to taste
- pinch of freshly grated nutmeg
- $3/4$ cup/90 g freshly grated Parmesan cheese, to serve

Stock: Place the chicken and beef in a large pan with the water. Bring to a boil and add the onion, leek, garlic, bay leaf, parsley, and salt. Simmer over low heat for about 2 hours. Drain and filter, reserving 2 quarts (2 liters) of stock to serve the cappellacci. • Prepare the pasta dough following the instructions on pages 9–11. Let rest for 30 minutes. • Filling: Melt the butter in a small saucepan and sauté the pork, sausage, turkey, prosciutto, and veal over medium heat for 5 minutes, or until lightly browned. • Remove from the heat and chop in a food processor. • Transfer to a bowl and add the egg and Parmesan. Season with salt, pepper, and nutmeg. • Divide the dough into 4 pieces. Roll it through the machine one notch at a time down to the thinnest setting. Cut the dough $1^{1}/4$-inch (3-cm) squares. • Form scant teaspoons of filling into small balls. Place one at the center of each piece of pasta and shape into cappellacci following the instructions on page 99. • Place the chicken stock in a large pan over high heat. Cover and bring to a boil. • Cook the pasta in batches in the boiling stock until al dente, about 3–4 minutes. • Sprinkle with Parmesan and serve hot.

Serves 6; Preparation: 45 minutes + time to make the pasta; Cooking: 2 hours 30 minutes; Level 3

Above: Cappellacci with eggplant and chocolate

Below: Cappellacci in chicken stock

CAPPELLETTI DI ZAFFERANO CON RICOTTA E FIORI CON PESCE AZZURRO

Saffron cappelletti with Ricotta cheese and zucchini flowers in seafood sauce

Pasta
- $1/2$ quantity plain fresh pasta dough (see chart on page 8)
- $1/4$ teaspoon powdered saffron dissolved in 1 tablespoon of water
- 2 tablespoons coarse sea salt (to cook the pasta)

Filling
- 4 tablespoons extra-virgin olive oil
- 12 zucchini/courgette flowers, cleaned and coarsely chopped
- salt and freshly ground white pepper to taste
- 14 oz/400 g Ricotta cheese, drained
- 4 tablespoons freshly grated young Pecorino cheese

Sauce
- 12 oz/350 g fresh anchovies, heads and bones removed
- 6 tablespoons extra-virgin olive oil
- 4 oz/125 g finely chopped white onion
- salt and freshly ground white pepper to taste
- 4 tablespoons dry white wine
- 1 tablespoon toasted pine nuts
- 2 tablespoons golden raisins/sultanas, soaked in warm water for 2 hours
- 4 zucchini/courgette flowers, cleaned and sliced, to garnish

Prepare the pasta dough, incorporating the saffron-flavored water, following the instructions on pages 9–11. Let rest for 30 minutes. • Filling: Heat the oil in a large skillet (frying pan) and sauté the zucchini flowers with a pinch of salt for 3 minutes. Remove from the skillet and drain on paper towels. Chop them finely. • Strain the Ricotta into a medium bowl and add the chopped zucchini flowers. Mix in the Pecorino and season with salt and pepper. Refrigerate until ready to use. • Sauce: Rinse the anchovies, dry well with paper towels, and chop into $3/4$-inch (2-cm) chunks. • Heat 3 tablespoons of oil in a saucepan and cook the onion with a pinch of salt over low heat for 10 minutes. • Pour in the wine and cook until evaporated. • Add the pine nuts and golden raisins and cook over medium heat for 3 minutes. • Heat the remaining oil in a large skillet and sauté the anchovies over high heat until lightly browned. Season with salt and pepper and add to the pan with the onion. • Keep the sauce warm until ready to serve. • Divide the pasta dough into 4 pieces. Roll it through the machine one notch at a time down to the thinnest setting. • Cut the dough into $2^1/2$-inch (6-cm) squares. • Place a walnut-sized blob of filling in the center of each square. Fold and seal the pasta into the classic cappelletti shape (with pointed pieces of pasta sticking out) following the instructions on page 99. • Place a large pan of water over high heat with the coarse sea salt. Cover and bring to a boil. • Cook the pasta in 2 batches in the boiling water until al dente, about 3 minutes. • Drain well. Spoon the anchovy sauce into individual serving dishes and add the pasta. • Garnish with the zucchini flowers and serve immediately.

Serves 4; Preparation: 1 hour + time to make the pasta; Cooking: 30 minutes; Level 3

TORTELLI CACIO E PERE

Cheese and pear tortelli

Pasta
- $1/2$ quantity plain fresh pasta dough (see chart on page 8)
- 1 teaspoon freshly ground white pepper
- 2 tablespoons coarse sea salt (to cook the pasta)

Filling
- $1^1/4$ cups/150 g coarsely grated Pecorino cheese
- 5 oz/150 g fresh Ricotta cheese, drained
- 1 small pear, peeled, cored, and coarsely grated
- 1 egg
- salt and freshly ground white pepper to taste

To serve
- 4 tablespoons coarsely grated Pecorino cheese
- 6 tablespoons melted butter
- freshly ground black pepper to taste

Prepare the pasta dough following the instructions on pages 9–11. Let rest for 30 minutes. • Filling: Mix the Pecorino, Ricotta, pear, egg, salt, and pepper in a medium bowl. • Divide the dough into 3 pieces. Roll it through the machine one notch at a time down to the second thinnest setting. • Cut the dough into $2^1/2$-inch (6-cm) squares. • Place a heaped teaspoon of filling onto the center of each square. Fold and seal the pasta into the classic cappelletti shape (with pointed pieces of pasta sticking out) following the instructions for cappelletti on page 99. • Place a large pan of water over high heat with the coarse sea salt. Cover and bring to a boil. • Cook the pasta in 2 or 3 batches in the boiling water until al dente, about 3–4 minutes. • Drain well and transfer to individual serving dishes. • Sprinkle with the Pecorino, drizzle with the butter, and grind with pepper. • Serve immediately.

Serves 4; Preparation: 1 hour 30 minutes + time to make the pasta; Cooking: 15 minutes; Level 3

Cheese and pear tortelli

RAVIOLI FRIULANI DOLCI
Sweet Friulian ravioli

Pasta
- 2 cups/300 g all-purpose/plain flour
- $^1/_2$ cup/125 ml warm water
- pinch of salt
- 2 tablespoons coarse sea salt (to cook the pasta)

Filling
- 4 tablespoons butter, cut up
- $3^1/_2$ oz/100 g finely chopped red onion
- salt and freshly ground black pepper to taste
- 14 oz/400 g mashed potatoes
- 1 teaspoon ground cinnamon
- 4 tablespoons golden raisins/sultanas, soaked in cold water for 2 hours
- 6 tablespoons finely chopped walnuts
- finely grated zest of $^1/_2$ lemon
- 1 teaspoon dried mint
- 1 tablespoon sugar
- 1 egg, lightly beaten

Sauce
- $^3/_4$ cup/90 g freshly grated smoked Ricotta
- 6 tablespoons melted butter

Prepare the pasta dough using the flour, water, and salt and following the instructions on pages 9–11. Let rest for 30 minutes. • Filling: Melt the butter in a medium saucepan. Cook the onion with a pinch of salt over low heat for 10 minutes. • Mix the mashed potatoes, onion, cinnamon, golden raisins, walnuts, lemon zest, mint, and sugar in a medium bowl. Season with salt and pepper and refrigerate until ready to use. • Divide the pasta dough into 4 pieces. Roll it through the machine one notch at a time down to the thinnest setting. Use a fluted round pastry or cookie cutter to cut into 3-inch (8-cm) disks. • Shape pieces of filling into balls the size of a walnut and place one at the center of each disk. Brush with beaten egg and fold over into a half-moon shape, pressing down around the edges to seal. Fold the edges back on themselves to make a decorative border. Place on a floured cloth until ready to cook. • Place a large pan of water over high heat with the coarse sea salt. Cover and bring to a boil. • Cook the pasta in batches in the boiling water until al dente, about 3–4 minutes. • Drain well and place in a heated serving dish. Sprinkle with the Ricotta and drizzle with the butter. • Serve immediately.

Serves 4; Preparation: 1 hour 30 minutes + time to make the pasta; Cooking: 1 hour; Level 3

PASTA PIENA
Filled pasta in meat stock

Pasta
- $^3/_4$ quantity plain fresh pasta dough (see chart on page 8)

Filling
- 10 oz/300 g Stracchino cheese (or other fresh creamy cheese)
- $1^1/_4$ cups/150 g freshly grated Parmesan cheese
- 1 egg
- finely grated zest of $^1/_2$ lemon
- 1 tablespoon finely chopped chives
- 1 tablespoon fine dry bread crumbs
- salt and freshly ground white pepper to taste

To serve
- $1^1/_4$ quarts/1.25 liters Meat stock (see page 97)
- 1 tablespoon finely chopped chives

Prepare the pasta dough following the instructions on pages 9–11. Let rest for 30 minutes. • Filling: Mix the Stracchino, Parmesan, egg, lemon zest, chives, and bread crumbs in a medium bowl. Season with salt and pepper and refrigerate until ready to use. • Divide the dough into 4 pieces. Roll it through the machine one notch at a time down to the second thinnest setting. • Spread 2 sheets of dough with a thin even layer of filling. Cover with the remaining sheets of dough and press down lightly with the rolling pin to make it stick. • Use a fluted pastry cutter to cut into strips about 1 inch (2.5 cm) wide, then cut into squares. • Place the stock over high heat. Cover and bring to a boil. • Cook the pasta in batches in the boiling stock until al dente, about 5 minutes. • Ladle the pasta and stock into individual bowls and sprinkle with the chives. • Serve immediately.

Serves 4; Preparation: 25 minutes + time to make the pasta; Cooking: 20 minutes; Level 2

Filled pasta in meat stock

RAVIOLI ALLA BIRRA
Ravioli with beer

Filling
- 14 oz/400 g stewing beef
- 7 oz/200 g finely chopped onion
- 3^1/$_2$ oz/100 g celeriac, cut in cubes
- 1 carrot, cut in cubes
- 2 cloves garlic, peeled and cut in half
- 1 inch/2.5 cm cinnamon stick
- 2 juniper berries
- 1 teaspoon tomato paste/purée
- 2 tablespoons extra-virgin olive oil
- 1^1/$_4$ cups/310 ml dark beer
- 2 eggs
- salt and freshly ground black pepper to taste
- 4 tablespoons freshly grated Parmesan cheese

Pasta
- ^{1}/$_2$ quantity plain fresh pasta dough (see chart on page 8)
- 2 tablespoons coarse sea salt (to cook the pasta)

Marinate the beef with the onion, celeriac, carrot, garlic, cinnamon, juniper berries, pepper, and beer in a bowl in the refrigerator for 12 hours. • Prepare the pasta dough following the instructions on pages 9–11. Let rest for 30 minutes. • Remove the meat from the marinade, dry well, and brown in a large skillet (frying pan) with the oil. • Bring the marinade to a boil and add the meat. • Stir in the tomato paste and season with salt. • Simmer over low heat for 2 hours, or until the meat is tender. • Remove the meat from the cooking liquids and let them cool. Chop the liquids in a food processor until smooth. • Chop the meat in a food processor and place in a bowl. Add the eggs and Parmesan and season with salt and pepper. Refrigerate until ready to use. • Divide the pasta dough into 4 pieces. Roll it through the machine one notch at a time down to the thinnest setting. • Cut the dough into 2^1/$_2$-inch (6-cm) disks with a smooth pastry cutter. • Place teaspoonfuls of filling in the center of each disk and fold the pasta over the filling in half-moon shapes, sealing the edges well. Place on a floured cloth until ready to cook. • Place a large pan of water over high heat with the coarse sea salt. Cover and bring to a boil. • Cook the pasta in the boiling water until al dente, about 3 minutes. • Drain the pasta well and place in a heated serving dish. • Spoon the reheated cooking liquids over the top. Sprinkle with the Parmesan and serve immediately.

Serves 4: Preparation; 30 minutes + 12 hours to marinate + time to make the pasta; Cooking: 20 minutes; Level 3

RAVIOLI DI RICOTTA E MENTA ALLE ZUCCHINE
Ricotta and mint ravioli with zucchini

Pasta
- ^{1}/$_2$ quantity plain fresh pasta dough (see chart on pages 00)
- 2 tablespoons coarse sea salt (to cook the pasta)

Filling
- 1 lb/500 g very fresh Ricotta cheese, drained of its whey
- ^{3}/$_4$ cup/90 g freshly grated Pecorino cheese
- 1 egg
- 2 tablespoons finely chopped mint
- salt and freshly ground white pepper to taste

Sauce
- 4 tablespoons extra-virgin olive oil
- 2 cloves garlic, finely chopped
- 1 lb/500 g zucchini/courgettes, cut in matchsticks
- 3 ripe tomatoes, peeled, seeds gently squeezed out, and coarsely chopped
- 1 tablespoon finely chopped parsley
- salt and freshly ground black pepper to taste
- 5 leaves fresh basil, torn

Prepare the pasta dough following the instructions on pages 9–11. Let rest for 30 minutes. • Filling: Strain the Ricotta into a bowl and mix in the Pecorino, egg, and mint. Season with salt and pepper. • Place the mixture in a pastry bag fitted with a smooth tip and refrigerate until ready to use. • Sauce: Heat the oil in a large skillet and sauté the garlic until it turns pale gold. • Add the zucchini and sauté over high heat for 15 minutes. • Add the tomatoes and parsley and cook for 2 minutes. Season with salt and pepper and stir in the basil. • Place a large pan of water over high heat with the coarse sea salt. Cover and bring to a boil. • Divide the pasta dough into 4 pieces. Roll each one through the machine one notch at a time down to the thinnest setting. Place two sheets of pasta on a floured work surface and pipe small blobs of filling all over, spacing them about 2 inches (5 cm) apart. Cover with the remaining sheets of pasta, pressing down gently with your fingertips among the blobs of pasta to seal. • Cut out disks about 1^1/$_2$ inches (4 cm) in diameter. • Carefully transfer to a floured cloth until ready to use. • Cook the pasta in the boiling water until al dente, about 2 minutes. Drain well and place in a serving dish. • Spoon the zucchini sauce over the top. Serve immediately.

Serves 4; Preparation: 45 minutes + time to make the pasta; Cooking: 45 minutes; Level 3

RAVIOLINI AL CEDRO
Ravioli with candied citron peel

Pasta
- $1/2$ quantity plain fresh pasta dough (see chart on page 8)
- 2 tablespoons coarse sea salt (to cook the pasta)
- $1^1/2$ tablespoons melted butter

Filling
- 3 oz/90 g candied citron peel, finely chopped
- $3^1/2$ oz/100 g ground almonds
- finely grated zest of $1/2$ lemon
- $3^1/2$ oz/100 g Ricotta cheese, drained
- 1 small egg
- salt and freshly ground white pepper to taste
- 6 tablespoons melted butter
- 1 tablespoon sugar
- pinch of freshly grated nutmeg

Prepare the pasta dough following the instructions on pages 9–11. Let rest for 30 minutes. • Filling: Place the citron peel, almonds, lemon zest, Ricotta, and egg in a medium bowl. season with salt and pepper and mix well. • Divide the pasta dough into 4 pieces. Roll it through the machine one notch at a time down to the thinnest setting. Cut the dough into long strips about $2^1/2$ inches (6 cm) wide. • Place balls of filling about the size of marbles down the strip of pasta leaving plenty of space between them. Cover the strips of pasta with other strips, pressing down between the filling and along the edges to seal. Use a fluted pastry cutter about 1 inch (2.5 cm) in diameter to cut out the ravioli. Carefully transfer the ravioli onto a lightly floured cloth until ready to cook. • Place a large pan of water over high heat with the coarse sea salt. Cover and bring to a boil. • Cook the pasta in the boiling water until al dente, about 2–3 minutes. • Drain well and transfer to a serving dish. • Drizzle with the butter, sprinkle with the sugar and nutmeg. • Serve immediately.

Serves 4; Preparation: 45 minutes + time to make the pasta; Cooking: 20 minutes; Level 3

RAVIOLI DEL VALDARNO
Ravioli from the Arno Valley

Sauce
- 5 tablespoons extra-virgin olive oil
- $3^1/2$ oz/100 g finely chopped red onion
- 2 oz/60 g finely chopped celery
- $3^1/2$ oz/100 g finely chopped carrot
- pinch of salt
- $1^1/2$ lb/750 g goose meat, boned and cut in 1-inch (2.5-cm) chunks
- 2 cloves garlic
- $2/3$ cup/180 ml dry red wine
- $1^1/4$ cups/310 g finely chopped canned tomatoes
- 2 cups/500 ml beef stock
- 1 tablespoon finely chopped parsley
- $3/4$ cup/90 g freshly grated Parmesan cheese

Pasta
- $3/4$ quantity plain fresh pasta dough (see chart on page 8)
- 2 tablespoons coarse sea salt (to cook the pasta)

Filling
- 1 lb/500 g Ricotta cheese, drained
- 2 tablespoons finely chopped parsley
- 1 clove garlic, finely chopped
- 1 egg

Sauce: Heat the oil in an earthenware casserole and add the onion, celery, carrot, and a pinch of salt. Cover and cook for 10 minutes. • Add the goose meat and garlic and sauté over high heat for 15 minutes. • Pour in the wine and cook until evaporated. Cook for 15 minutes more. • Add the tomatoes, scant 1 cup (200 ml) of stock, parsley, salt, and pepper. Cover and cook over low heat for 1 hour, or until the meat is tender and the sauce has reduced. Add more stock if the sauce dries out. • While the sauce is cooking, prepare the pasta dough following the instructions on pages 9–11. Let rest for 30 minutes. • Filling: Strain the Ricotta into a large bowl and mix in the egg and parsley. Season with salt and pepper. Place in a pastry bag and refrigerate until ready to use. • Divide the pasta dough into 6 pieces. Roll it through the machine one notch at a time down to the second thinnest setting. • Pipe blobs of filling the size of marbles on half of each sheet of pasta, leaving about 1 inch (2.5 cm) between each blob. Fold the other half of the pasta over the top, pressing down between the blobs of filling to seal (see page 100). Use a fluted pastry cutter to cut out square or rectangular ravioli. Press the edges of the ravioli with the tines (prongs) of a fork to decorate and seal well. • Carefully transfer to a floured cloth until ready to cook. • Place a large pan of water over high heat with the coarse sea salt. Cover and bring to a boil. • Cook the pasta in the boiling water until al dente, about 4 minutes. • Drain well and arrange in layers, alternating with the sauce, on a heated serving dish. • Serve immediately.

Serves 6; Preparation: 1 hour 30 minutes + time to make the pasta; Cooking: 2 hours 30 minutes; Level 3

SPIGHE
Braids with asparagus and Gorgonzola filling

Pasta
- $3/4$ quantity plain fresh pasta dough (see chart on page 8)
- 2 tablespoons coarse sea salt (to cook the pasta)

Filling
- 10 oz/300 g asparagus
- 1 cup/250 ml chicken or vegetable stock
- $3^1/2$ oz/100 g Gorgonzola cheese
- 1 egg
- 2 tablespoons fine dry bread crumbs
- 4 tablespoons freshly grated Parmesan cheese
- salt and freshly ground white pepper to taste

Sauce
- scant 1 cup/200 ml dry white wine
- 2 scallions/spring onions, finely chopped
- 2 tablespoons butter, cut up

Prepare the pasta dough following the instructions on pages 9–11. Let rest for 30 minutes. • Filling: Separate the tips of the asparagus from the stalks. Blanch the tips and stalks in salted boiling water for 2 minutes. Set the tips aside. Peel the stalks and cut into $1/2$-inch (1-cm) pieces). • Heat the stock in a small saucepan and add the asparagus stalks. Cook for 5 minutes, or until tender (depending on the thickness of the stalks). Drain and chop the stalks in a food processor until puréed. • Mix the Gorgonzola in a small bowl with a fork until creamy. • Add the puréed asparagus cream, egg, bread crumbs, Parmesan, salt, and pepper. • Divide the dough into 4–5 pieces. Roll it through the machine one notch at a time down to the second thinnest setting. Cut the dough into disks about 4 inches (10 cm) in diameter. There should be about 18 disks. • Use a tablespoon to place some filling in the center of each disk. Begin to seal the "braids" by pulling a small piece of pasta down across the filling, then pulling small pieces of pasta alternately from left and right in a braiding movement until the filling is completely covered. • Place the "braids" on a clean dry cloth and sprinkle with hard wheat flour. • Place a large pan of water over high heat with the coarse sea salt. Cover and bring to a boil. • Sauce: Place the wine, scallions, and butter in a small saucepan and cook until reduced by half. • Strain the sauce and add the asparagus tips. • Cook the pasta in the boiling water until al dente, about 3–4 minutes. • Drain the pasta well and transfer to individual serving dishes. Drizzle with the sauce and serve immediately.

Serves 4–6; Preparation: 1 hour + time to make the pasta; Cooking: 30 minutes; Level 3

RAVIOLI DI RICOTTA AL PECORINO
Ravioli with Ricotta and Pecorino cheese

Pasta
- $1^1/3$ cups/200 g all-purpose/plain flour
- 1 egg
- about 4 tablespoons cold water
- 2 tablespoons coarse sea salt (to cook the pasta)

Filling
- 10 oz/300 g fresh Ricotta cheese, drained
- 4 tablespoons melted butter
- 3 tablespoons freshly grated Parmesan cheese
- 3 tablespoons cooking juices from roast meat (or stock)
- 1 egg
- pinch of freshly grated nutmeg
- salt and freshly ground white pepper to taste

Sauce
- 4 tablespoons butter
- 3 tablespoons cooking juices from roast meat (or stock)
- scant 1 cup/200 ml fresh cream
- 7 oz/200 g fresh Pecorino cheese, in thin flakes

Prepare the pasta dough using the flour, egg, and water and following the instructions on pages 9–11. Let rest for 30 minutes. • Filling: Mix the Ricotta, butter, Parmesan, cooking juices, egg, nutmeg, salt, and pepper in a medium bowl. Refrigerate until ready to use. • Divide the pasta dough into 4 pieces. Roll it through the machine one notch at a time down to the thinnest setting. Cut the dough into long strips about $2^1/2$ inches (6 cm) wide. • Place teaspoons of filling down the center of half the strips, leaving about 1 inch (2.5 cm) between each blob of filling. Cover the strips of pasta with other strips, pressing down between the filling and along the edges to seal. Use a fluted pastry cutter to cut out the ravioli. Carefully transfer the ravioli to a floured cloth until ready to cook. • Place a large pan of water over high heat with the coarse sea salt. Cover and bring to a boil. • Sauce: Melt the butter with the cooking juices in a small saucepan. Cook for 4 minutes. • Pour in the cream and simmer for 10 minutes. • Cook the pasta in the boiling water until al dente, about 2–3 minutes. • Drain well and transfer to a serving dish. • Pour the sauce over the top and sprinkle with the Pecorino. • Serve immediately.

Serves 4; Preparation: 30 minutes + time to make the pasta; Cooking: 20 minutes; Level 3

Above: Braids with asparagus and Gorgonzola filling

Below: Ravioli with Ricotta and Pecorino cheese

RAVIOLI CON PATATE ALLA BOTTARGA

Potato ravioli with bottarga

Bottarga is a Mediterranean delicacy made from the eggs of tuna or mullet which have been salted, pressed, and dried in the sun. In Italy, bottarga is especially typical of Sardinia, but it is also used in France, where it is known as *poutargue*, in Turkey, where it is called *putago*, in Greece, where it is known as *avotáracho*, and in Tunisia, where it is called *boutargue*. It can be bought in dry pieces or powdered form.

Pasta
- $1/2$ quantity plain fresh pasta dough (see chart on page 8)
- 2 tablespoons coarse sea salt (to cook the pasta)

Sauce
- 7 tablespoons butter, cut up
- 2 oz/60 g bottarga (pressed salted tuna or mullet roe), grated or in powdered form
- 2 cloves garlic, lightly crushed with the back of a knife but whole

Filling
- 1 lb/500 g floury white potatoes
- $3/4$ cup/90 g freshly grated Parmesan cheese
- 4 tablespoons butter, cut up
- 1 tablespoon finely chopped parsley
- $1/4$ teaspoon freshly grated nutmeg
- 1 clove garlic, finely chopped
- salt and freshly ground white pepper to taste

Prepare the pasta dough following the instructions on pages 9–11. Let rest for 30 minutes. • Sauce: Melt the butter in a small saucepan. Remove from the heat and add the bottarga. Stir well and set aside for 30 minutes. • Filling: Cook the potatoes in their skins in salted, boiling water for 25 minutes, or until tender. • Let cool, then slip off the skins. • Mash the potatoes in a large bowl with the Parmesan, butter, parsley, nutmeg, garlic, salt, and pepper. When this mixture is smooth and well blended, place in a pastry bag. • Divide the dough into 3 pieces. Roll it through the machine one notch at a time down to the second thinnest setting. Cut the dough into disks about 3 inches (8 cm) in diameter. • Pipe about 1 teaspoon of filling onto the center of each disk of pasta. Fold each piece of dough in half over the pasta (see page 96) and seal in a half-moon shape. Press the edges down gently with the tines (prongs) of a fork to seal, taking care not to puncture the pasta with the fork. • Place the ravioli on a clean dry cloth and sprinkle with hard wheat flour. Do not leave the ravioli for more than an hour before cooking, especially if your kitchen is humid. The potato filling can soften the pasta too much so that it breaks when you lift the ravioli away from the cloth for cooking. • Place a large pan of water over high heat with the coarse sea salt. Cover and bring to a boil. • Cook the pasta in the boiling water until al dente, about 3–4 minutes. • Reheat the bottarga with the garlic. Discard the garlic. • Drain the pasta well and transfer to a serving dish. Drizzle with the sauce and serve immediately.

Serves 4; Preparation: 45 minutes + time to make the pasta; Cooking: 40 minutes; Level 3

RAVIOLI DI RUCOLA E CAGLIATA

Ravioli with arugula and curd

If you don't have curd on hand, you can make your own by boiling 1 quart (1 liter) of milk. Add 1 tablespoon of fresh lemon juice and remove from the heat. Set aside to curdle. Pour into a sieve lined with a clean cloth. Close the cloth around the curd and let drain for 2 hours. You will need about 4 oz (125 g) for this recipe.

Pasta
- $1/2$ quantity plain fresh pasta dough (see chart on page 8)
- 2 tablespoons coarse sea salt (to cook the pasta)

Filling
- $1^1/4$ lb/625 g Swiss chard leaves, stalks removed
- 10 oz/300 g arugula/rocket
- 4 oz/125 g curd cheese
- $3/4$ cup/90 g freshly grated Parmesan cheese
- 2 egg yolks
- salt and freshly ground white pepper to taste

Sauce
- 4 tablespoons basil sauce (see *Lasagne with basil sauce*, page 79)
- 4 tablespoons extra-virgin olive oil

Prepare the pasta dough following the instructions on pages 9–11. Let rest for 30 minutes. • Filling: Boil the Swiss chard and arugula in salted water for about 10 minutes. Drain well, squeeze out the excess moisture, and chop it finely. • Transfer to a bowl and add the curd, Parmesan, and egg yolks. Season with salt and pepper and refrigerate until ready to use. • Divide the pasta into 4 pieces. Roll each piece through the machine one notch at a time down to the second thinnest setting. Cut half the pasta into 2-inch (5-cm) squares and half into 2-inch (5-cm) disks. • Place 1 teaspoon of filling at the center of each square and cover with a disk of pasta. Press down on the edges to seal. • Place a large pan of water over high heat with the coarse sea salt. Cover and bring to a boil. • Cook the pasta in the boiling water until al dente, about 3 minutes. • Sauce: Mix the pesto with the oil and 2 tablespoons of cooking water. • Drain the pasta and transfer in layers to a heated serving dish. Spoon a little of the sauce over each layer. • Serve hot.

Serves 4; Preparation: 1 hour + time to make the pasta; Cooking: 30 minutes; Level 3

Potato ravioli with bottarga

RAVIOLI AL MAIALE

Pork ravioli

Pasta
- 1 1/3 cups/200 g all-purpose/plain flour
- 1 egg
- about 4 tablespoons cold water
- 2 tablespoons coarse sea salt (to cook the pasta)

Filling
- 1 1/2 tablespoons butter, cut up
- 10 oz/300 g lean pork, cut in 1-inch (2.5-cm) cubes
- 2 tablespoons dry Marsala wine
- 3 1/2 oz/100 g prosciutto/Parma ham, sliced
- 1 oz/30 g fresh bread crumbs
- 1 egg
- 2 tablespoons freshly grated Parmesan cheese
- salt and freshly ground black pepper to taste

Sauce
- 1 1/2 tablespoons butter, cut up
- 3 1/2 oz/100 g peeled, cored, and thinly sliced Golden Delicious apples
- 1 scallion/spring onion, finely chopped
- 4 tablespoons dry Marsala wine
- scant 1/2 cup/100 ml beef stock
- salt and freshly ground black pepper to taste

Prepare the pasta dough using the flour, egg, and water and following the instructions on pages 9–11. Let rest for 30 minutes. • Filling: Melt the butter in a large skillet (frying pan) and sauté the pork over medium heat for 4–5 minutes, or until lightly browned. • Add the Marsala and cook until evaporated. • Remove from the heat and let cool, reserving the cooking juices. • Transfer to a food processor with the prosciutto and bread crumbs and chop finely. • Transfer the mixture to a bowl and add the egg, Parmesan, salt, and pepper. Refrigerate until ready to use. • Divide the pasta dough into 4 pieces. Roll it through the machine one notch at a time down to the thinnest setting. • Form teaspoons of filling into balls the size of marbles and place on half of each sheet of pasta, leaving about 1 inch (2.5 cm) between each blob. Fold the other half of the pasta over the top, pressing down between the blobs of filling to seal. •. Use a fluted pastry cutter to cut out ravioli measuring about 1 1/4 inches (3 cm) square. Carefully transfer to a floured cloth until ready to cook. • Place a large pan of water over high heat with the coarse sea salt. Cover and bring to a boil. • Sauce: Heat the cooking juices reserved from the filling with the butter in a small saucepan. Add the apples and scallion and cook over low heat for 5 minutes. • Add the Marsala and cook until evaporated. • Pour in the stock, season with salt and pepper, and cook over low heat for 5 minutes, or until the sauce has reduced by half. • Chop in a food processor, then return to the skillet over low heat. • Cook the pasta in the boiling water until al dente, about 2–3 minutes. • Drain

well and transfer to the skillet with the sauce. Cook for 1–2 minutes, scooping a little sauce over the top. • Serve immediately.

Serves 4: Preparation: 1 hour 30 minutes + time to make the pasta; Cooking: 45 minutes; Level 3

ROTOLO CON RICOTTA E BIETOLA

Swiss chard and Ricotta roll

Pasta
- 3/4 quantity plain fresh pasta dough (see chart on page 8)
- 2 tablespoons coarse sea salt (to cook the pasta)

Filling
- 2 tablespoons butter, cut up
- 1 1/4 lb/625 g cooked Swiss chard, squeezed dry and finely chopped
- 10 oz/300 g fresh Ricotta cheese
- 3/4 cup/90 g freshly grated Parmesan cheese
- 1 teaspoon finely grated lemon zest
- salt and freshly ground white pepper to taste
- 3 1/2 oz/100 g melted butter

Prepare the pasta dough following the instructions on pages 9–11. Let rest for 30 minutes. • Filling: Melt the butter in a large skillet (frying pan) and sauté the Swiss chard for 10 minutes. • Season with salt and remove from the heat. Let cool. • Strain the Ricotta and mix in the cooled Swiss chard with the Parmesan, lemon zest, salt, and pepper. • Divide the dough into 3 pieces. Roll it through the machine one notch at a time down to the second thinnest setting. Trim the pieces to obtain neat rectangles. • Spread the sheets of dough with even layers of filling, leaving a border around the edges. Roll the sheets of pasta up carefully and wrap in clean pieces of muslin (cheesecloth). Tie the ends with kitchen string. • Place a large pan of water over high heat. Cover and bring to a boil. • Cook the pasta in the boiling water for 20 minutes. • Remove the rolls from the water and unwrap the muslin. Cut in thick slices and drizzle with the melted butter. • Serve immediately.

Serves 6; Preparation: 1 hour + time to make the pasta; Cooking: 30 minutes; Level 3

Swiss chard and Ricotta roll

TORTELLI
Basic tortelli

Pasta
- $1/2$ quantity plain fresh pasta dough (see chart on page 8)
- 2 tablespoons coarse sea salt (to cook the pasta)

Filling
- 14 oz/400 g Ricotta cheese, drained
- 7 oz/200 g cooked, squeezed, finely chopped spinach
- 1 egg
- $1/2$ cup/60 g freshly grated Parmesan cheese
- finely grated zest of $1/2$ lemon
- salt and freshly ground black pepper to taste

Prepare the pasta dough following the instructions on pages 9–11. Let rest for 30 minutes. • Filling: Mix the Ricotta, spinach, egg, Parmesan, lemon zest, salt, and pepper in a large bowl. Transfer to a pastry bag fitted with a smooth tip. • Divide the dough into 4–5 pieces. Roll it through the machine one notch at a time down to the thinnest or second thinnest setting (if you like your pasta a little thicker, as in many regional dishes). • Cut the dough into disks about 3 inches (8 cm) in diameter. • Pipe a blob of filling about the size of a walnut onto the center of each disk. Fold and seal the pasta into the classic tortelli shape following the instructions for Cappelletti on page 98. • Place a large pan of water over high heat with the coarse sea salt. Cover and bring to a boil. • Cook the tortelli in 2 or 3 batches in the boiling water until al dente, about 3–4 minutes. • Drain the pasta well and transfer a heated serving dish. • Spoon the sauce of your choice over the top and serve immediately.

Serves 4; Preparation: 30 minutes + time to make the pasta; Cooking: 20 minutes; Level 3

RAVIOLI CON PECORINO E PERE
Ravioli with pears and Pecorino cheese

Pasta
- $1/2$ quantity plain fresh pasta dough (see chart on page 8)
- 2 tablespoons coarse sea salt (to cook the pasta)

Filling
- 3 firm, ripe pears (Kaiser are good)
- juice of $1/2$ lemon
- scant 1 cup/100 ml water
- 1 tablespoon sugar
- $3/4$ cup/90 g freshly grated Pecorino cheese
- freshly ground black pepper to taste

Sauce
- $31/2$ oz/100 g butter
- 1 sprig marjoram
- pinch of salt
- $1/2$ cup/60 g freshly grated aged Pecorino cheese
- $1/2$ teaspoon ground cinnamon

Prepare the pasta dough following the instructions on pages 9–11. Let rest for 30 minutes. • Filling: Peel the pears and drizzle with the lemon juice to prevent them from turning black. Cut them in small cubes. • Place the water in a medium saucepan with the sugar and pears. Cover with a piece of waxed paper (directly on the pears) and simmer gently for 20 minutes, stirring occasionally. The pears should be tender but not mushy. • Divide the pasta dough into 4 pieces. Roll it through the machine one notch at a time down to the thinnest setting. Cut into pieces about 2 inches (5 cm) square. • Place a teaspoon of the filling, Pecorino, and a pinch of pepper at the center of half of all the squares of pasta. Place a square of pasta on top of each and press down around the edges to seal. If liked, use a fluted pastry cutter to create decorative borders. Carefully transfer to a floured cloth until ready to use. • Place a large pan of water over high heat with the coarse sea salt. Cover and bring to a boil. • Sauce: Melt the butter in a small saucepan with the marjoram and salt. • Cook the pasta in the boiling water until al dente, about 3–4 minutes. Drain well and place in a serving dish. • Drizzle with the sauce, sprinkle with the Pecorino, and dust with the cinnamon. Serve immediately.

Serves 4; Preparation: 45 minutes + time to make the pasta; Cooking: 30 minutes; Level 3

RAVIOLI DI NASELLO E CAPESANTE
Seafood ravioli

Pasta
- 1¹/₃ cups/200 g all-purpose/plain flour
- 1 egg
- about 4 tablespoons cold water
- 2 tablespoons coarse sea salt (to cook the pasta)

Filling
- ¹/₂ onion
- 1 bay leaf
- 3 white peppercorns
- 2 sprigs parsley
- salt and freshly ground white pepper to taste
- 8 oz/250 g hake, chopped
- 3 tablespoons garlic-flavored extra-virgin olive oil
- 10 oz/300 g gurnard fillets, chopped
- 1 tablespoon dry vermouth
- 1 tablespoon sherry
- 4 tablespoons all-purpose/plain flour
- 7 oz/200 g shelled scallops, cut in ¹/₄-inch/0.5-cm cubes
- 1¹/₂ tablespoons butter
- 1 egg
- 1 tablespoon finely chopped parsley

Sauce
- 4 tablespoons garlic-flavored extra-virgin olive oil
- 7 oz/200 g mullet fillets
- 7 oz/200 g shelled shrimp, cut in half lengthwise
- 12 oz/350 g peeled and chopped tomatoes
- 2 tablespoons dry vermouth
- 2 tablespoons butter
- 1 tablespoon finely chopped parsley

Prepare the pasta dough using the flour, egg, and water and following the instructions on pages 9–11. Let rest for 30 minutes. • Filling: Fill a medium saucepan with cold water and add the onion, bay leaf, white peppercorns, and sprigs of parsley. Season with salt, bring to a boil, and cook for 20 minutes. • Add the hake and cook over low heat for 5 minutes. • Drain the hake, remove the skin and bones, and strain into a bowl through a sieve. • Heat 1 tablespoon of the garlic-flavored oil in a large skillet (frying pan). Add the gurnard and cook over high heat for 2 minutes. • Pour in the vermouth and sherry and cook until evaporated. • Remove from the heat and finely chop the fish and cooking juices. • Dust the scallops lightly with the flour. • Melt the butter in a small skillet and sauté the scallops for 4 minutes. Season with salt and remove from the heat. • Combine the hake, gurnard, and scallops in a medium bowl. Season with salt and pepper and add the remaining garlic-flavored oil. Stir in the egg and parsley. • Divide the pasta dough into 4 pieces. Roll it through the machine one notch at a time down to the thinnest setting. • Cut into 3-inch (8-cm) wide strips. • Place half tablespoons of filling down the center of each strip,

keeping them about 1 inch (2.5 cm) apart. Fold the pasta over the top and press down to seal. Use a fluted pastry cutter to cut into ravioli about 2 x 1-inch (5 x 3-cm). • Place a large pan of water over high heat with the coarse sea salt. Cover and bring to a boil. • Sauce: Heat the garlic-flavored oil in a large skillet and add the mullet and shrimp. Cook over high heat for 2 minutes. Add the vermouth and cook until evaporated. • Stir in the tomato, season with salt and pepper, and cook for 2 minutes. • Cook the pasta in the boiling water until al dente, about 3 minutes. • Drain the pasta and transfer to the skillet with the sauce. Add the butter and 4 tablespoons of cooking water. • Sprinkle with the parsley and serve immediately.

Serves 4: Preparation: 2 hours + time to make the pasta; Cooking: 1 hour; Level 3

TORTELLI FRITTI RIPIENI DI ZUCCA
Fried pumpkin-filled tortelli

Pasta
- 1¹/₃ cups/200 g all-purpose/plain flour
- 2 tablespoons extra-virgin olive oil
- 4–5 tablespoons water
- salt to taste

Filling
- 5 oz/150 g winter squash or pumpkin, baked in the oven, and mashed
- 5 oz/150 g Italian sausage meat
- 2 oz/60 g black truffles, finely chopped
- 4 tablespoons freshly grated Parmesan cheese
- pinch of freshly grated nutmeg
- salt and freshly ground black pepper to taste
- 1–2 cup(s)/250–500 ml olive oil, for frying

Prepare the pasta dough using the flour, oil, and water and following the instructions on pages 9–11. Let rest for 30 minutes. • Filling: Mix the pumpkin and sausage in a medium bowl. Stir in the truffles, Parmesan, and nutmeg. Season with salt and pepper. • Divide the pasta dough into 4 pieces. Roll it through the machine one notch at a time down to the thinnest setting. • Cut the dough into 3 x 12-inch (8 x 30-cm) strips. • Place a scant tablespoon of filling at one end of a strip and fold a corner of pasta over the top to form a triangle. Fold the triangle four more times down the strip and seal the edges. Continue until all the pasta and filling have been used. • Heat the oil in a deep-fryer and fry the tortelli in batches until golden brown. • Drain on paper towels and serve hot.

Serves 4; Preparation: 45 minutes + time to make the pasta; Cooking: 20 minutes; Level 3

RAVIOLINI IN BRODO CON FOIE GRAS E TARTUFO

Little ravioli in stock with pâté and truffles

Pasta
- 1 1/3 cups/200 g all-purpose/plain flour
- 1 very fresh large egg
- about 4 tablespoons cold water
- 2 tablespoons coarse sea salt (to cook the pasta)

Filling
- 7 oz/200 g foie gras pâté (bloc de foie gras), cut in small cubes
- 1 black truffle, weighing about 1 oz/30 g, cleaned and finely chopped
- 1 1/4 quarts/1.25 liters Chicken stock (see page 116)
- scant 1 cup/100 ml dry white Port

Prepare the pasta dough using the flour, egg, and water and following the instructions on pages 9–11. Let rest for 30 minutes. • Divide the pasta dough into 4 pieces. Roll it through the machine one notch at a time down to the thinnest setting. Cut into disks about 1 1/4 inches (3 cm) in diameter. • Place a cube of pâté and a pinch of truffle at the center of half of all the disks of pasta. Cover with the remaining disks, pressing down around the edges to seal. Carefully transfer to a floured cloth until ready to use. • Place the chicken stock in a medium saucepan and bring to a boil. Add the raviolini and cook until al dente, about 1 minute. • Serve hot with the stock.

Serves 6; Preparation: 30 minutes + time to make the pasta; Cooking: 20 minutes; Level 3

RAVIOLONE A STRISCE

Large striped ravioli

These eyecatching ravioli are fairly complicated and time-consuming to make. However, they can be prepared ahead of time and frozen.

Pasta
- 1 quantity plain fresh pasta dough (see chart on page 8)
- 1/3 quantity aromatic (herb) pasta dough (see chart on page 8)
- 1/3 quantity colored (tomato) pasta dough (see chart on page 8)
- 1/3 quantity black pasta dough (see chart on page 8)
- 2 tablespoons coarse sea salt (to cook the pasta)

Filling
- 1 lb/500 g Ricotta cheese
- 2 eggs
- 1 1/2 cups/180 g freshly grated Parmesan cheese
- salt and freshly ground black pepper to taste

Sauce
- 2 lb/1 kg g cauliflower, head cut in small florets, stems in small cubes
- 2 tablespoons white wine vinegar
- salt and freshly ground white pepper to taste
- 4 tablespoons extra-virgin olive oil
- 2 sprigs marjoram, finely chopped, + extra to garnish
- 2 sprigs wild fennel, finely chopped, + extra to garnish

Prepare the four types of pasta following the instructions on pages 9–11. Let rest for 30 minutes. • Filling: Mix the Ricotta in a large bowl until smooth and creamy. Add the eggs and Parmesan and season with salt and pepper. • Transfer to a pastry bag and refrigerate until ready to use. • Divide the plain pasta dough into 4–6 pieces. Roll each piece through the machine one notch at a time down to the second thinnest setting. Cut into sheets about 5 inches (13 cm) square. • Divide the other pasta doughs into 2 and roll each piece through the machine one notch at a time down to the thinnest setting. Cut into 1/2 x 5 inches (1 x 13 cm) strips. Place the strips of colored pasta on the plain pasta and roll through the machine following the instructions on page 67. You should have 16 squares of striped pasta. • Divide the filling into 8 and spread over 8 pieces of pasta, leaving a 3/4-inch (2-cm) border around the edges. Cover with the remaining pieces of pasta, pressing down on the edges to seal. If necessary, dampen the edges of pasta with a little cold water to seal better. Place the ravioli on a clean cloth sprinkled with durum wheat flour until ready to cook. • Sauce: Bring enough water to cover the cauliflower to a boil in a medium saucepan. Add the vinegar, a pinch of salt, and the cauliflower and cook until tender, about 15 minutes. Drain and chop in a food processor with the oil and herbs.• Place a large pan of water over high heat with the coarse sea salt. Cover and bring to a boil. • Cook the pasta in batches in the boiling water until al dente, about 4 minutes. • Drain carefully and place in individual serving dishes with the cauliflower sauce. • Serve immediately.

Serves 8; Preparation: 1 hour + time to make the pasta; Cooking: 40 minutes; Level 3

Large striped ravioli

RAVIOLO DI RADICCHIO IN BRODO DI FAGIANO
Ravioli with radicchio filling in pheasant stock

The pheasant stock may need to be clarified to remove all extra fat and impurities. To clarify, add the egg white to the stock and return to the heat, stirring gently until the stock just begins to steam. At that point stop stirring and wait for the egg white to appear on the surface filtering any impurities. Simmer for a few minutes, then strain through a clean cloth taking care not to break the egg white.

Pheasant stock
• 1 pheasant (excluding the breast, see below)
• 1 shallot
• white part of 1 leek
• 2 teaspoons black peppercorns
• 1 bay leaf
• 2 juniper berries
• small piece of cinnamon stick
• $1/2$ stalk celery
• $1/2$ carrot
• 1 sprig fresh thyme
• salt to taste
• 1 egg white (optional, see above)
• 1 pheasant breast, sautéed in butter and a little dry Marsala wine
Pasta
• 1 quantity ravioli pasta dough (see chart on page 8)
• 2 tablespoons coarse sea salt (to cook the pasta)
Filling
• 4 tablespoons extra-virgin olive oil
• $1/2$ cup/125 ml dry red wine
• 10 oz/300 g red radicchio (preferably Treviso), cut in julienne strips
• $3/4$ cup/90 g freshly grated Parmesan cheese
• $3^1/2$ oz/100 g fresh Ricotta cheese
• 2 tablespoons freshly grated Ricotta salata cheese
• $1/4$ teaspoon freshly grated nutmeg
• salt and freshly ground white pepper to taste

Pheasant stock: Place the pheasant (excluding the breast) in a medium pan of cold water and bring to a boil. Skim off any scum and add the shallot, leek, peppercorns, bay leaf, juniper berries, cinnamon, celery, carrot, thyme, and salt. Partially cover and simmer for 1 hour. • Remove from the heat and let cool. Skim the fat off the surface. • Chop the cooked pheasant breast in julienne strips and add to the stock. • Prepare the pasta dough following the instructions on pages 9–11. Let rest for 30 minutes. • Filling: Heat the oil in a large skillet and sauté the radicchio for 5 minutes, or until softened. • Pour in the wine and cook until evaporated. • Remove from the heat and let cool. Drain, if necessary, and chop finely. • Transfer the radicchio mixture in a bowl and add the Parmesan, both Ricotta cheeses, the nutmeg, salt,

and pepper. • Divide the dough into 5 or 6 pieces. Roll it through the machine one notch at a time down to the second thinnest setting. Cut the dough into star-shaped pieces about 1 inch (3 cm) wide. (If you do not have small star-shaped molds to cut the dough just make square or rectangular small ravioli.) • Place a large pan of water over high heat with the coarse sea salt. Cover and bring to a boil. • Cook the pasta in the boiling water until al dente, about 2–3 minutes. • While the pasta is cooking, reheat the pheasant stock. • Drain the pasta and add to the stock. Serve hot.

Serves 4; Preparation: 1 hour + time to make the pasta; Cooking: 1 hour 30 minutes; Level 3

TORTELLI RICOTTA, ARANCIO E BOTTARGA
Tortelli with Ricotta and orange filling in bottarga sauce

Pasta
• $1/2$ quantity plain fresh pasta dough (see chart on page 8)
• 2 tablespoons coarse sea salt (to cook the pasta)
Filling
• 14 oz/400 g Ricotta cheese, drained
• 10 oz/300 g cooked white beans (cannellini, white kidney beans)
• finely grated zest of 1 orange
• 1 egg, lightly beaten
• 3 tablespoons dry bread crumbs
• salt and freshly ground white pepper to taste
Sauce
• $3^1/2$ oz/100 g butter
• 2 oz/60 g bottarga, thinly sliced

Prepare the pasta dough following the instructions on pages 9–11. Let rest for 30 minutes. • Filling: Strain the Ricotta, removing all extra moisture, and place in a large bowl. • Chop the beans in a food processor and add to the bowl with the orange zest, egg, and bread crumbs. Season with salt and pepper. • Transfer to a pastry bag fitted with a wide, smooth tip. • Divide the pasta dough into 4 pieces. Roll it through the machine one notch at a time down to the thinnest setting. • Cut the dough into $2^1/2$-inch (6-cm) disks. • Pipe marble-sized blobs of filling into the center of each disk and fold the pasta over the filling in half-moon shapes, sealing the edges well. Place on a floured cloth until ready to cook. • Place a large pan of water over high heat with the coarse sea salt. Cover and bring to a boil. • Sauce: Melt the butter in a small saucepan and add the bottarga. Let rest for 10 minutes. • Cook the pasta in the boiling water until al dente, about 3 minutes. • Drain the pasta well and place in individual serving dishes. • Spoon the sauce over the top and serve immediately.

Serves 4; Preparation: 45 minutes + time to make the pasta; Cooking: 20 minutes; Level 3

Ravioli with radicchio filling in pheasant stock

TORTELLINI BIANCHI E ROSSI
Red and white tortellini

Pasta
- 1/4 quantity plain fresh pasta dough (see chart on page 8)
- 1/4 quantity colored (tomato) pasta dough (see chart on pages 8)
- 2 tablespoons coarse sea salt (to cook the pasta)

Filling
- 1 cup/125 g freshly grated Parmesan cheese
- 6 tablespoons dry bread crumbs
- 1 egg
- 1 1/2 tablespoons melted butter
- pinch of freshly grated nutmeg
- salt and freshly ground white pepper to taste

Sauce
- 2 tablespoons butter, cut up
- 7 oz/200 g cooked, finely chopped spinach
- 4 tablespoons all-purpose/plain flour
- 2 1/2 cups/625 ml Chicken stock (see page 116)
- salt and freshly ground white pepper to taste

Prepare the pasta doughs following the instructions on pages 9–11. Let rest for 30 minutes. • Filling: Place the Parmesan, bread crumbs, egg, butter, nutmeg, salt, and pepper in a small bowl and mix well. Transfer to a pastry bag. Refrigerate until ready to use. • Divide each piece of pasta into 2 pieces. Roll it through the machine one notch at a time down to the thinnest setting. • Cut the dough into 1-inch (2.5-cm) squares. • Pipe small marble-sized blobs of filling into the center of each square and shape into tortellini following the instructions on page 96. Place on a floured cloth until ready to cook. • Place a large pan of water over high heat with the coarse sea salt. Cover and bring to a boil. • Sauce: Melt the butter in a medium saucepan and sauté the spinach for 3 minutes. • Add the flour and cook for 3 minutes. • Pour in the stock and season with salt and pepper. Bring to a boil and cook over low heat for 15 minutes, stirring often. • Remove from the heat and chop finely in a food processor. Reheat, then ladle into individual serving dishes. • Cook the pasta in the boiling water until al dente, about 2 minutes. • Drain the pasta well and place in the dishes over the sauce. • Serve immediately.

Serves 4; Preparation: 1 hour + time to make the pasta; Cooking: 30 minutes; Level 3

RAVIOLI ALLA RUSSA
Ravioli Russian-style

Pasta
- 2 cups/300 g all-purpose/plain flour
- 1 egg
- about 1/3 cup/100 ml warm water

Filling
- 10 oz/300 g ground/minced beef
- 2 onions, finely chopped
- 1 tablespoon water
- salt and freshly ground black pepper to taste

To serve
- 2/3 cup/150 ml sour cream
- 1 tablespoon finely chopped dill

Prepare the pasta dough using the flour, egg, and water and following the instructions on pages 9–11. Let rest for 30 minutes. • Filling: Chop the beef and onion in a food processor. Transfer to a bowl and stir in the water. Season with salt and pepper. • Divide the pasta dough into 4 pieces. Roll it through the machine one notch at a time down to the thinnest setting. Cut into disks about 4 inches (10 cm) in diameter. • Place a 1/2 tablespoon of filling at the center of all the disks of pasta. Fold the pasta over to form half-moon shapes and press down around the edges to seal. Carefully transfer to a floured cloth until ready to use. • Place a large pan of water over high heat with the coarse sea salt. Cover and bring to a boil. • Cook the pasta in the boiling water for 8–10 minutes. Drain well and place in a serving dish. • Mix the sour cream and dill and pour over the pasta. • Serve immediately.

Serves 4; Preparation: 1 hour + time to make the pasta; Cooking: 20 minutes; Level 3

Ravioli Russian-style

TORTELLI DI VERDURA
Vegetable tortelli

Pasta
- $1/2$ quantity plain fresh pasta dough (see chart on page 8)
- 2 tablespoons coarse sea salt (to cook the pasta)

Filling
- 12 oz/350 g Swiss chard, cooked and squeezed dry
- $3^1/2$ oz/100 g boiled carrots
- $3^1/2$ oz/100 g boiled celery
- $3^1/2$ oz/100 g boiled red onions
- 2 tablespoons butter, cut up
- 1 egg
- $1^1/2$ oz/45 g fresh bread crumbs, soaked in 3 tablespoons cream
- 4 tablespoons freshly grated Parmesan cheese
- finely grated zest of 1 lemon
- salt and freshly ground black pepper to taste

Sauce
- 4 tablespoons extra-virgin olive oil
- 1 clove garlic, finely chopped
- 10 oz/300 g cabbage, shredded
- scant 1 cup/200 ml water
- 4 tablespoons freshly grated Parmesan cheese

Prepare the pasta dough following the instructions on pages 9–11. Let rest for 30 minutes. • Filling: Chop the Swiss chard, carrots, celery, and onions finely. Melt the butter in a large skillet (frying pan) and cook the chopped vegetables over low heat for 5 minutes. • Remove from the heat and place in a bowl. Add the egg, bread crumbs, Parmesan, and lemon zest. Season with salt and pepper. • Sauce: Heat the oil and garlic in a large saucepan. Add the cabbage and water and season with salt. Cover and cook over medium-low heat until the cabbage is mushy, about 40 minutes. • Divide the pasta dough into 4 pieces. Roll it through the machine one notch at a time down to the thinnest setting. • Place teaspoons of filling evenly spaced on two sheets of pasta and cover with the other two sheets of pasta, pressing down lightly with your fingertips between the blobs of filling. Cut into squares. Place on a floured cloth. • Place a large pan of water over high heat with the coarse sea salt. Cover and bring to a boil. • Cook the pasta in batches in the boiling water until al dente, about 3 minutes. • Drain the pasta and place in the saucepan with the cabbage sauce. • Cook over low heat for 5 minutes. • Sprinkle with the Parmesan and serve.

Serves 4; Preparation: 30 minutes + time to make the pasta; Cooking: 1 hour 30 minutes; Level 3

RAVIOLI BICOLORE
Two-toned ravioli

Pasta
- $1/2$ quantity aromatic (saffron) pasta dough (see chart on page 8)
- $1/2$ quantity colored (spinach) pasta dough (see chart on page 8)
- 2 tablespoons coarse sea salt (to cook the pasta)

Filling
- 2 tablespoons butter, cut up
- 7 oz/200 g fresh salmon fillets, chopped
- 2 tablespoons dry Martini
- 2 egg yolks
- 2 tablespoons fresh cream
- 2 tablespoons fine dry bread crumbs
- 2 tablespoons freshly grated Parmesan cheese
- 1 tablespoon finely chopped dill
- salt and freshly ground white pepper to taste

Sauce
- 1 lb/500 g fresh porcini (or other wild mushroom), cleaned, stalks and caps separated
- 5 tablespoons garlic-flavored extra-virgin olive oil
- 1 tablespoon finely chopped dill
- 1 tablespoon all-purpose/plain flour
- $1^1/3$ cups/300 ml Fish stock (see page 97)
- salt and freshly ground white pepper to taste
- 4 tablespoons freshly grated Parmesan cheese (optional)

Prepare the pasta doughs following the instructions on pages 9–11. • Filling: Melt the butter in a large skillet (frying pan) over high heat. Add the salmon and sear well. • Add the Martini and cook until evaporated. • Let cool, then chop in a food processor. • Transfer to a bowl and add the egg yolks, cream, bread crumbs, Parmesan, and dill. Season with salt and pepper. • Transfer to a pastry bag. • Sauce: Cut the mushroom stalks in $1/2$-inch (1-cm) cubes. Chop the heads in $1/4$-inch (6 mm) slices. • Heat the garlic-flavored oil in a large skillet and add the mushrooms and a pinch of salt. Cover and cook over medium heat for 10 minutes. • Add the flour and cook over high heat for 2 minutes. Pour in the stock. Season with salt and pepper, cover, and cook over low heat for 15 minutes. • Remove from the heat and add the dill. • Divide both pasta doughs in half. Roll each piece through the machine one notch at a time down to the thinnest setting. Cut each piece into eight 3-inch (8-cm) squares. • Pipe a tablespoon of filling onto half of the pieces of pasta of both colors. Cover each square with a piece of pasta of the other color. • Place on a clean floured. • Place a large pan of water over high heat with the coarse sea salt. Cover and bring to a boil. • Cook the pasta in batches in the boiling water until al dente, about 3 minutes. • Drain carefully and place in the skillet with the mushroom sauce. • Serve with the Parmesan, if liked.

Serves 4; Preparation: 1 hour + time to make the pasta; Cooking: 45 minutes; Level 3

Two-toned ravioli

DOMINO DI CASTAGNE E FUNGHI
Double ravioli with chestnut and mushroom filling

Pasta
- $^3/_4$ quantity plain fresh pasta dough (see chart on page 8)
- 2 tablespoons coarse sea salt (to cook the pasta)

Mushroom filling
- 2 tablespoons extra-virgin olive oil
- 1 clove garlic, peeled and lightly crushed
- 10 oz/300 g potatoes
- 10 oz/300 g porcini mushrooms, cleaned and coarsely chopped
- 1 sprig mint
- salt and freshly ground black pepper to taste
- $1^1/_2$ tablespoons butter, cut up

Chestnut filling
- 7 oz/200 g chestnuts
- salt to taste
- 1 bay leaf
- 2 oz/60 g Ricotta cheese, drained
- $^1/_2$ egg
- 4 tablespoons freshly grated Parmesan cheese

Sauce
- 6 tablespoons butter, cut up
- 1 clove garlic
- 1 teaspoon finely chopped mint
- 1 teaspoon fresh thyme leaves
- 1 teaspoon finely chopped fresh rosemary leaves
- salt to taste

Prepare the pasta dough following the instructions on pages 9–11. • Mushroom filling: Boil the potatoes in salted, boiling water until tender. • Drain and slip off the skins. Transfer to a bowl and mash until smooth. • Heat the oil and garlic in a medium saucepan and add the mushrooms and mint. Cover and cook over low heat and cook for 30 minutes. • Season with pepper. Discard the garlic and chop in a food processor. Mix the chopped mushroom mixture and butter to the mashed potatoes. • Chestnut filling: Use a sharp knife to pierce the chestnuts. Boil in salted water for 10 minutes. • Drain and peel, removing both the outer and inner skins. • Place the chestnuts in a saucepan and cover with water. Season lightly with salt and add the bay leaf. Cover and cook for 30 minutes, or until tender. • Drain, remove the bay leaf, and transfer to a bowl. Mash, adding the Ricotta, egg, and Parmesan. • Divide the dough into 4 pieces. Roll it through the machine one notch at a time down to the second thinnest setting. Cut into strips $2^1/_2$ inches (6 cm) wide. • Place alternate tablespoons of mushroom and chestnut filling down the center of half the strips, spacing them 1 inch (2.5 cm) apart. Cover with another strip of pasta, pressing down between the blobs with your fingertips. Use a fluted pastry cutter to cut out 2 x 4 inches (5 x 10 cm) rectangles. • Place a large pan of water over high heat with the coarse sea salt. Cover and bring to a boil. • Cook the pasta in batches in the boiling water until al dente, about 2–3 minutes. • Drain and place in a heated serving dish. • Sauce: Mix the butter, garlic,

mint, thyme, rosemary and salt in a small saucepan over low heat. Pour over the pasta and serve.

Serves 4; Preparation: 2 hours + time to make the pasta; Cooking: 1 hour 15 minutes; Level 3

MEZZELUNE
Half moons

Pasta
- $1^1/_3$ cups/200 g all-purpose flour
- 1 egg
- about 4 tablespoons cold water

Filling
- $3^1/_2$ oz/100 g day-old bread, crusts removed
- scant $^1/_2$ cup/100 ml dry white wine
- 2 artichokes
- juice of 1 lemon
- 3 tablespoons extra-virgin olive oil
- $^1/_2$ clove garlic, finely chopped
- 1 tablespoon finely chopped mint
- salt and freshly ground black pepper to taste
- 1 quart/1 liter cold water
- 1 small onion, finely chopped
- 2 oz/60 g smoked ham
- 2 cups/250 g freshly grated Parmesan cheese
- 1 egg

Sauce
- 3 tablespoons melted butter
- 4 tablespoons extra-virgin olive oil
- 1 tablespoon finely chopped mint
- salt to taste

Prepare the pasta dough using the flour, egg, and water following the instructions on pages 9–11. • Filling: Soak the bread in the wine. • Clean the artichokes and place in a bowl of cold water with the lemon juice. • Slice thinly and place in a skillet (frying pan) with 2 tablespoons of oil, garlic, mint, salt, and pepper. Pour in the water and cover and cook for 10 minutes, or until the artichokes are tender. • In a small skillet, sweat the onion with the remaining oil and salt for 10 minutes. • Add the ham and cook for 4 minutes. • Chop both mixtures with a large knife. • Place the mixture in a bowl and mix in the Parmesan and egg. Season with salt and pepper. • Place a large pan of water over high heat with the coarse sea salt. Cover and bring to a boil. • Divide the dough into 3 pieces. Roll through the machine one notch at a time down to the thinnest setting. Cut into 2-inch (5-cm) disks. • Place walnut-sized balls of filling at the center of each disk of pasta. Fold into half moon shapes. • Cook the pasta in batches in the boiling water until al dente, about 2–3 minutes. Drain and transfer to a serving dish. • Sauce: Mix the butter, oil, mint, and salt in a small bowl and pour over the pasta. • Serve hot.

Serves 4: Preparation: 1 hour + time to make the pasta; Cooking: 40 minutes; Level 3

Above: Double ravioli with chestnut and mushroom filling

Below: Half moons

Index